AD Biography
Kern Jer 1953

P9-CCT-064

Ewen, David, 1907 – 1985. The story of Jerome
Kern   9000313362

9000313362

The Story of Jerome Kern

By DAVID EWEN in this same series

THE STORY OF GEORGE GERSHWIN

TALES FROM THE VIENNA WOODS:
The Story of Johann Strauss

HAYDN: A Good Life

THE STORY OF IRVING BERLIN

THE STORY OF ARTURO TOSCANINI

JEROME KERN

by DAVID EWEN

⊱⊰⊱⊰⊱⊰⊱⊰⊱⊰⊱⊰⊱⊰⊱⊰⊱⊰⊱⊰⊱⊰⊱⊰⊱⊰⊱⊰⊱⊰⊱⊰⊱⊰⊱⊰

The Story of

JEROME KERN

⊱⊰⊱⊰⊱⊰⊱⊰⊱⊰⊱⊰⊱⊰⊱⊰⊱⊰⊱⊰⊱⊰⊱⊰⊱⊰⊱⊰⊱⊰⊱⊰⊱⊰⊱⊰

HOLT, RINEHART AND WINSTON
NEW YORK

Library of Congress Catalog Card Number:
52–13066

Published, March, 1953
Second Printing, November, 1958
Third Printing, June, 1962

92625–0513

PRINTED IN THE UNITED STATES OF AMERICA

"Genius is surely not too extravagant a word for him. . . .
He left us rare treasures."

Editorial in the New York *Herald Tribune*
(NOVEMBER 12, 1945)

Contents

INTRODUCTION *All the Things He Was* 3

ONE *"A Node in the Vibrations of the 19th Century"* 13

TWO *One Piano—Two Hundred Pianos* 19

THREE *Not Defeat, but Victory* 23

FOUR *Songs for Sale* 29

FIVE *The First Shows* 35

SIX *Success* 41

SEVEN *A Great Deal of Luck* 49

EIGHT *And a Great Deal of Talent* 55

NINE Show Boat *Is Born* 63

Contents

TEN   Show Boat *Is Produced*   69

ELEVEN   Show Boat *Is Immortal*   75

TWELVE   *Good-by, Broadway*   79

THIRTEEN   *Hello, Hollywood*   85

FOURTEEN   *"Can't Help Lovin' Dat Man"*   89

FIFTEEN   *Jerome Kern—of Carnegie Hall*   95

SIXTEEN   *Paris: 1942*   103

SEVENTEEN   *Good-by, Mr. Kern*   107

EIGHTEEN   *"He Jes' Keeps Rollin' Along"*   113

APPENDIXES

1. A Select List of Broadway Productions for Which Jerome Kern Wrote the Complete Score   119

2. A Select List of Broadway Productions in Which Jerome Kern Songs Were Interpolated   123

3. Motion Pictures for Which Jerome Kern Wrote the Complete Score   127

4. Motion Pictures in Which Jerome Kern Songs Were Interpolated   129

5. The Fifty Greatest Songs of Jerome Kern   131

6. Recommended Recordings of Music by Jerome Kern   135

INDEX   143

The Story of Jerome Kern

All the Things He Was

THIS is a book about an American composer. He never wrote an opera, symphony, string quartet, or sonata. The only music he produced for the concert hall are two orchestral works which, truth to tell, belong with his less important achievements.

This composer—his name is Jerome Kern—owes his immense fame exclusively to the many songs he created for the Broadway theater and the Hollywood motion-picture screen. He was a composer of *popular* music. He was also a great composer, a genius.

To describe a popular composer as either "great" or a "genius" will startle only those who assume a snobbish attitude toward popular music. These people place a boundary between the serious and the popular in music, but there is really no such dividing line. In the last analysis, music is either good or bad, and the style or

3

idiom employed does not determine the quality. A dull and stuffy opera is not preferable to *Show Boat,* nor is a pedantic and uninspired German *Lied* worthier than a song like "Smoke Gets in Your Eyes." If a composer has genius, his genius will penetrate his best works, be they symphonies or popular tunes. By the same token, his music will survive whether he intended it for Carnegie Hall or for the Broadway musical stage.

Musical history is on the side of those who admire good popular music. For such music has always been esteemed respectfully by the greatest European musicians. Haydn, Beethoven, Mozart, and Schubert all created popular music when they wrote Ländler, German dances, waltzes, and other varieties of Austrian folk dances. When Bach produced chorales he was writing the music of the masses, and for the masses. Offenbach fashioned music for the cancan, that disreputable Parisian dance of the Second Empire. Brahms, Verdi, Gounod, and many others regarded Vienna's waltz king, Johann Strauss II, as their equal. Other important European composers of the recent past and the present —men like Satie, Debussy, Ravel, Stravinsky, Milhaud— have employed the popular idioms of American music with the most serious intent and often with immense artistic success.

A story is told that when the great Wagnerian prima donna of another day, Mme. Johanna Gadski, signed a contract to sing at the Palace Theatre, in New York— a vaudeville theater—some of her admirers expressed amazement and scorn that she should be willing to appear on such a stage. Mme. Gadski answered proudly, "Any theater in which *I* appear becomes at once a temple of art." It is possible to echo Mme. Gadski's sentiments regarding composers like Johann Strauss II of the nineteenth century and Jerome Kern of the twentieth. These composers are not demeaning themselves when they write waltzes or popular songs; on the contrary, any musical medium, however mean, becomes good art when men of great talent devote themselves to it. It is worth remembering that Johann Strauss II wrote his music for the café house and the popular theater in the nineteenth century, but in our day his works are often heard in the symphony hall (in performances by our leading orchestras under the foremost conductors), on records, and in the opera house.

Jerome Kern wrote his first published song in 1905, and his first complete score for the Broadway theater in 1911. Up to 1945, the end of a highly productive existence, he wrote innumerable songs and scores and achieved unprecedented success. Few careers in Tin Pan Alley match his for sustained accomplishment and uninterrupted recognition. With a million-copy sale an achievement reached by few songs, Kern was able to produce more than a dozen which sold more than two million copies each. He was also the collaborator in more successful musical-comedy and motion-picture produc-

5

tions than any other living composer—with the possible exception of Irving Berlin.

But it is not his success alone which has given him his importance. Much more important than that was his role in bringing artistic importance to the American popular song, his share in changing the destiny of the American musical theater.

Up to about 1900 the popular song in America was usually a naïve and cliché-ridden commodity. Formulas governed the stilted melodies, which had stereotyped, evenly balanced phrases. The tonic-subdominant accompaniments and the rhythms were invariably conventional. The musical expression was static: sentimental ballads or vaudeville ditties or dialect songs all followed accepted patterns. At times there emerged a composer, blessed with melodic sensitivity, who could produce poignant music even with such stultifying formulas. Stephen Foster was such a composer. So was James A. Bland, author of "Carry Me Back to Old Virginny." Later on, Victor Herbert was still another, though his style was within the European traditions rather than the American. But in Union Square where in 1880 and 1890 the popular song became an industry (and in Tin Pan Alley where a decade later it grew into a mighty Trust) originality was held suspect and fastidiously avoided. Composers of popular songs were invariably illiterate musicians who played the piano with a single finger and had to dictate the music to an amanuensis before it could be put down on paper.

6

A trained musician like Victor Herbert (who was capable of writing symphonies and concertos) was an exception.

Tin Pan Alley's atmosphere was stifling; it smothered talent and originality. If it had not been for rapidly changing social forces, it would not have been likely that a Jerome Kern could emerge, survive, and flourish.

Before the twentieth century the singing of popular songs was an integral part of our social life. On many an evening, family and friends would gather around the parlor piano (or player piano) to sing the songs of the day. The greatest single market for sheet music and song books was then the American family. Since the ordinary member of the average family was not particularly sophisticated in music, these songs had to be simple, formal, and conventional.

It was only just before the close of the nineteenth century and in the first years of the twentieth, that parlor singing lost favor as a form of family amusement. Theatrical entertainments were becoming popular, and the theater-going habit was being cultivated. If people continued singing popular songs, this practice was more of a personal diversion than a social or communal habit. When Americans sought musical pleasures they preferred to *listen* to songs rather than to *sing* them.

The popular song was now written with an eye toward the trained performer rather than the amateur. Consequently these songs could become more complex in technique, more independent in structure, without losing a market.

With Kern, the popular song was emancipated from its bondage to clichés and formulas. He was, to be sure, not the only one to bring this development about. There was Irving Berlin, who wrote his first songs and first became famous during the same period when Kern became known. And after Irving Berlin and Jerome Kern, there was George Gershwin.* But Kern was one of the earliest, and one of the most important, composers to bring an altogether new approach to the song of Tin Pan Alley. He came to song-writing with the technical equipment acquired as a student of serious music. With his innate freshness, vitality, charm, beauty of ideas, musical inventiveness, and originality, he brought an enriched harmony, a variety of rhythm, an understanding of counterpoint, and a structural logic. The enchantment of his best songs stems from his skillful use of devices taught him at the conservatory. The intriguing change of tempo in "You're Here and I'm Here," the adventurous use of harmony in "They Didn't Believe Me," the unusual intervallic structure in "All the Things You Are," the mobility of lyric line in "Look for the Silver Lining," the inevitability of design of "Smoke Gets in Your Eyes," the unorthodox accompaniment to "Magic Melody," the unusual melodic structure

* See *The Story of George Gershwin* (1943) and *The Story of Irving Berlin* (1950) in this series of biographies.

8

of "Bill"—and one could go on indefinitely!—betray the hand of a true artist.

He carved his songs as scrupulously and fastidiously as other composers do a symphony or a sonata. Though he wrote a great deal, he was always a most methodical craftsman, a painstaking workman who was rarely satisfied with what he had just written and who was always restless in his search for that satisfaction. Kern worked over every detail of a song until it had that inevitability —and that feeling of spontaneity—which we encounter in all great music. Kern always considered the popular song a worthy medium for any composer willing to bring to it the fullest resources of serious music. One of his many contributions was that he taught us, too, to respect and admire the popular song.

But Kern's importance does not rest exclusively on his songs. He was also one of the most significant pioneers in the American musical theater. Today, our musical theater has arrived at that point of evolution and development where it could yield such distinguished folk products as *Oklahoma!* and *South Pacific*. Kern, more than any other single composer, helped to bring this about. Richard Rodgers, the composer of the scores for both *Oklahoma!* and *South Pacific*, acknowledged his debt to Kern in the New York *Times*:*

Along with my love of Jerome Kern's music there

* October 7, 1951.

is a feeling of real gratitude. This was the man whose *Very Good, Eddie,* I saw at least a dozen times in one season. . . . The influence of such a hero on such a hero worshiper is not easy to calculate, but it was a deep and lasting one. His less successful musical comedies were no less important to a listener of thirteen or fourteen. I know that for a large part of one winter most of my allowance was spent in the balcony of the Maxine Elliott Theatre listening to the score of *Love o' Mike.*

Before Kern's time, the American musical comedy was as stilted, as much a slave to convention, as the popular song. Tradition dictated that the book serve merely as an excuse for songs, dances, and the comedy; it was not expected to have any intrinsic interest or any literary significance. The American musical comedy inherited some of the less desirable attributes of the European operetta: the tendency to exploit extravagant sets and costumes and casts; the preference for impossible situations in some make-believe and unreal setting; the emphasis on the dance at the expense of the dramatic action. Thus the American musical comedy was a loosely knit organism lacking coherence, logic, or realism. If the tunes were appealing, if the *décor* was colorful, if the chorus girls were attractive, if the comedy was amusing—and if the net result was good entertainment—the functions of the musical theater had been realized. Art belonged elsewhere. But this was before Kern entered and dominated the field.

His first important contribution was to divorce the American musical comedy from the European operetta. He did this first with a series of intimate musicals in the middle 1910's which came to be known as the "Princess Theatre Shows." His next revolution was to endow musical comedy with fresh character portrayals, genuine dramatic interest, piquant folk flavor. He did this in *Show Boat*. Then in *Music in the Air* and *The Cat and the Fiddle* he injected an even greater innovating spirit—a concern for unusual plots, an avoidance of hackneyed musical-comedy routines, and a continual enrichment of musical writing—which brought the American musical theater to full maturity.

This, then, is the story of an American composer who wrote some of the greatest and most successful songs of our generation. This is also the story of an American composer who revolutionized the American musical theater.

It is a story worth telling.

CHAPTER ONE

"A Node in the Vibrations of the 19th Century"

NEW YORK'S Sutton Place, which lies in the upper Fifties near the East River, is today a study in contrasts. Some of New York's most famous actors, writers, musicians, publishers, and financiers live there in elegant duplex and terrace apartments. But only a stone's throw away from these handsome residences lie slum areas.

In the closing decades of the nineteenth century, Sutton Place was a neighborhood for neither the very rich nor the very poor. It was a center for the city's brewery industry; but interspersed among these brewery buildings were respectable apartment houses where middle-class families lived.

The Kerns were such a middle-class family.

Henry and Fanny Kern, the father and mother, were both Americans by birth. He was of German extraction; she came from Bohemian stock. They had three children, all boys.

As president of a street-sprinkler association which had the concession to water the city streets, Henry Kern made a good living. Level-headed and materialistic (with a greater respect for, than acquaintance with, cultural things) he saw to it that the family was provided with the comforts and luxuries that made for gracious living.

Culture was the province of his wife Fanny. It was she who introduced good music into the household. Long before she was married she had aspired to be a concert pianist. She had demonstrated enough talent to give substance to her ambition. But marriage, and after that the raising of three children, frustrated her plans completely. Her girlhood dreams were forgotten long ago, but not her immense love for music and her devotion to the piano.

She made a calculated attempt to instill in each of her sons a love for good music. Continually she played for them the works of Beethoven, Chopin, Liszt, stopping now at a beautiful lyric phrase and now at an impressive harmony to direct the attention of her sons to it. Even before the boys had learned to read or write they were given instruction at the piano. Later on in life, Jerome Kern often recalled with nostalgic pleasure the little impromptu concerts which he, his mother, and his brother used to give in the Kern living room.

14

Jerome Kern was born on January 27, 1885, a day described by the well-known writer and critic, Alexander Woollcott, as "a node in the vibrations of the 19th century—a lull in the hubbub of history." He was the most musical of the three Kern children; it did not take long for the mother to recognize this fact. The ease with which he learned his piano lessons, and his enthusiasm, soon inspired in her the hope that she might some day realize her own frustrated ambitions in her son. She engaged a local piano teacher for Jerome so that he might profit by more experienced instruction than she could give him. The boy made such excellent progress that the teacher soon joined the boy's mother in accepting as a truth that Jerome must be directed toward a career as a professional musician.

Meanwhile there was a change of scene for the family. When Jerome was ten years old, his father gave up his street-sprinkling concession for an even more profitable venture, a merchandising house in Newark, New Jersey. In 1895 the Kerns moved to Newark.

Jerome continued his piano study with private teachers in Newark, while pursuing his academic education in the public schools. After completing elementary school, he entered the Newark High School. He had, by this time, made sufficient progress in his music studies to be able to play a prominent role in the musical activities at school. He was often called upon to play the piano; he was the official organist at the school assemblies; he helped to write and prepare the music for the annual school show. He was crazy about music and interested in little else. A quiet, self-centered boy, he did not make friends easily and was uncomfortable with the rowdy games of the city streets. In music he found escape—and adventure.

His teachers at Newark High School referred to him as "the little musical genius." Half out of admiration for his obvious aptitude for music, half out of affection for his gentle and lovable nature, they were tolerant to his complete and undisguised lack of interest in and dedication to any study removed from music. "I didn't have to study," he recalled later in life. "The teachers let me get away with a lot."

Once graduated, he was ready to renounce academic study for good. His mother was an ally in his wish to concentrate on music exclusively. But his father, a practical man, was hostile to the idea. He pointed out that a boy without a college education could hope for little in life. As for music—who ever made a living out of music? Father Kern, after all, had acquired enough of a smattering of musical information from his wife to be able to summon devastating arguments to prove his point. Did not Mozart die in a pauper's grave? Did not Schubert earn less during his entire lifetime than a janitor does in a single month?

"You're no Mozart, and you're no Schubert," Father Kern told his son with finality. "What, then, *can* you expect? Do you want to become one of those neighborhood piano teachers who get twenty-five cents a lesson?

Or, maybe, one of those starving long-hair composers who write pieces nobody wants to play or listen to?"

Father Kern was warming up to his subject. His arguments grew more persuasive. "If you don't want to go to college, that's a mistake you'll regret the rest of your life. But nobody can force you to go. If your heart and your mind are not in your studies you'll only be wasting the four years. But if you give up college you must turn to something practical, something that will provide you with a living. You can go into business with me, learn it from the ground up. I didn't do too badly for myself. Some day you'll be able to take over the business completely. But *music!—*" and Father Kern did not conceal that his disgust was too great for him to find the proper words with which to complete the sentence.

Fanny knew how to handle her husband. While his tirade went on she said nothing and motioned to her son to remain silent, too. Once the father's anger had been spent, and the flow of his arguments reduced to a trickle, Fanny could bring him around to her way of thinking.

"Give the child a chance to do what he wants, Henry," she now pleaded softly. "There's plenty of time to make a businessman out of him. In a year or two you can take him in with you. But first let the child go ahead with his music."

Fanny had her way. With a shrug of his shoulders, Father Kern conceded defeat. He could not deny that

17

Jerome was still a bit young to go into business. What harm could there be in letting him study music for a while? But in a year or so, Father Kern said emphatically, the boy would have to do some serious thinking about his future.

CHAPTER TWO

One Piano — Two Hundred Pianos

JEROME KERN enrolled in the New York College of Music. His teachers there included Paolo Gallico (father of the now well-known writer, Paul Gallico) and Alexander Lambert. He also soon supplemented this study with private lessons in harmony and theory from Dr. Austin Pierce.

He was an industrious student and possessed of an alert intelligence. Like the other dreamers who attended the New York College of Music he aspired to become, some day, the creator of symphonies and operas. Meanwhile he was learning to use the tools of his future trade.

Like the other dreamers at the conservatory, he had another ambition as well: to go to Europe to continue his music study there. In those years, the finishing touches to a musical education were always applied by European teachers. No self-respecting American musician regarded his training complete without some final study in Europe.

But Father Kern soon smothered such a dream. After all, the father had permitted the boy to indulge his passion in music for more than a year. The time for a final decision had arrived. Jerome Kern was seventeen years old. At seventeen, Father Kern said, a young man had to begin planning his future. "And that future," the father said firmly, "is not in music."

What the father had specifically in mind was for Jerome to enter his merchandising house and begin his apprenticeship without delay.

This time Father Kern would not be swayed by his wife. He had made up his mind, and there was not much that Fanny or Jerome could do about it. Besides, the year or so that Jerome had concentrated on music had proved one fact to the mother: Jerome had aptitude for music and a love for it; but he was no genius. He played the piano tolerably well, but he was most certainly not of virtuoso caliber. Nor was he particularly outstanding as a composer. The pieces he wrote for class, and sometimes for his own pleasure, were correct and in good taste; but that was about all that could be said for them.

If Jerome had been a blazing light at the New York College of Music there would have been powerful arguments with which to defeat Father Kern's purpose. As it was, Fanny realized sadly, Jerome had best yield to his father's wishes and try his hand at business.

In the summer of 1902 Jerome Kern started working

for his father. That association virtually began, and definitely ended, with a single transaction.

One of his first assignments was to go to New York City to buy two pianos. An enterprising salesman in one of the piano shops convinced him that each individual piano came at a cheaper price when bought in wholesale lots. Consequently, the total profit from the sale of many pianos was virtually a windfall, compared to the mere pittance realized through the sale of only one or two pianos. It was simple arithmetic, the salesman pointed out. "Take two hundred pianos and I'll be able to chop off twenty-five dollars from the price of each one. You'll be saving five thousand dollars!" The argument made sense to Jerome. Besides, the spell of salesmanship was irresistible to a young and inexperienced buyer. Jerome placed an order for two hundred pianos.

The deal at first almost ruined his father's business, since the pianos had to be paid for in cash. When Father Kern recovered from both his anger and his shock, he was faced with an inescapable truth. Whatever else his son might be, he was no businessman. After this sad experience with two hundred pianos, only a fool would entrust him with the running of a large and flourishing business. Sadly the father realized that, for the time being at any rate, it was wiser and less expensive to permit Jerome to continue studying music. He could even go to Europe if he wanted to!

There was a happy epilogue to this story.

His warehouse overcrowded with unsalable pianos

and his bank account depleted to the vanishing point, Father Kern had to evolve an attractive installment-plan scheme whereby families of modest income could afford to buy his pianos. While Jerome was in Europe, entering upon a professional career in music, Father Kern sold all his pianos this way and realized a huge profit for the Kern establishment. The boy's blunder had, after all, proved to be a business coup.

CHAPTER THREE

Not Defeat, But Victory

JEROME KERN left for Europe in the fall of 1903. He stayed abroad two years. He wandered about a great deal, absorbing the sights and assimilating new experiences with all the gusto of a wide-eyed tourist. He heard more music than ever before in his life. He undertook some study of harmony and composition in Heidelberg with private teachers. He also made some attempts at writing serious works in the large forms.

But what he did most of all was to take stock of himself.

Whither Jerome Kern?—he must have asked himself time and again as he traveled restlessly from one European city to another, almost as if expecting the answer in one of those places. His aborted attempts at composing provided evidence that his creative talent was more modest than both his love and his enthusiasm.

He could not fool himself on that point. His intermittent periods of study in Europe further emphasized his shortcomings; had, indeed, filled him with such a feeling of frustration that he had to discontinue lessons altogether. And yet the determination to make music his lifework never faltered. It was the only field in which he had received any training, and it was still his only all-abiding interest. But if he was not to become a serious composer—and if he had already definitely eliminated the concert stage—in which direction should he proceed? The disturbing question would give him no peace.

Accident finally provided the answer.

He had come to London very low in funds and with the determination not to ask his father for more. He had to find a job. He haunted the theatrical offices in London for some kind of work that could put his musical training to use. Only his inflexible determination to find such an opening, and to fill no other, made him continue the search after numerous rejections. But eventually he did find something. At that time musical shows in London used songs by unknown composers as opening numbers, paid for with a trifling fee. Since theater audiences came habitually late, few ever heard this opening music. The producers felt that anything serviceable could fill in the time before the main attraction.

The office of the American producer, Charles K. Frohman, then producing such musicals in London, needed the services of a composer able to write these inconsequential numbers and willing to accept a modest fee for his work. Kern was engaged. It was not much of an assignment. The income he received was less than that of a bank clerk. And the author of the music remained anonymous and could hardly expect to use these assignments as a stepping-stone to recognition. But for Kern, who needed any kind of a paying job badly and who was beginning to despair of ever finding a musical assignment, this opportunity seemed heaven-sent.

At that, this insignificant and poorly paid work was the turning point in his life. For the first time it provided him with a destination. Until now, he had regarded himself as a serious musician who must succeed with the writing of large works, for which he was completely out of his depth. But he was soon made to recognize that there was another world of music for which he was suited by temperament, training, and talent: that of popular music. Thus, unlike Irving Berlin and George Gershwin (who had gravitated naturally to popular music from their boyhood days on, knowing from the very first, and with unwavering conviction, that this was where their strength lay), Kern had come upon his future vocation more by accident than design. From the moment he wrote his first piece for the London theater he knew that he had found his lifework.

In that job in the Frohman office, Kern served an all-important apprenticeship. He gathered important experiences. The work brought him into the theater for the first time as an active (though still humble) collaborator. By having to write pieces of music tailor-made for stage specifications, he was learning valuable lessons from which the future composer of musical-comedy scores would profit greatly. That job also launched him officially on his career as a composer of popular songs. One of the items he wrote for the London shows became his first published song, "How'd You Like to Spoon with Me?" with lyrics by Edward Laska. It was published in the United States in 1905, after being interpolated in a Broadway show, *The Earl and the Girl*, starring Eddie Foy.

One of the young men who worked in the Frohman office was an aspiring writer by the name of P. G. Wodehouse. The name is now famous, for subsequently Wodehouse achieved an immense success as the writer of whimsical novels, among them such perennial favorites as *Leave It to Psmith* and *The Inimitable Jeeves*. In 1904, as an employee in the Frohman office, Wodehouse was twenty-three years old (four years Kern's senior) and was already writing pieces for the London newspapers. But like Kern he, too, was still uncertain about his future.

One day Wodehouse showed Kern some lyrics he had written. Diffidently he asked the young composer if they were good enough to be set to music. Kern said he liked them very much and stuffed them in his pocket. The next day he showed Wodehouse the melodies he had written to his words. It was the first time that anybody had provided tunes to his words; Wodehouse listened with star-eyed amazement as Kern played the songs for him.

Then he said wistfully, "You know, Jerry, some day we will both become famous—you as a composer, and I as a writer. When that happens we must work together as Mr. Words and Mr. Music!"

Young dreamers often make such wistful remarks to each other. Probably both Wodehouse and Kern would have been shocked, in 1904, if they could have known that some day the two of them would, indeed, become famous, and what was more, would work as collaborators.

By the time Kern returned to the United States in 1905, he had completely abandoned his youthful ambition to become a serious composer. He had by now convinced himself that the field of popular music was well worth cultivating and that it was here that his very special musical gifts could be put to fullest advantage. The difficult thing would be to sell the idea to his mother. For, from the moment Kern gave up business to return to music study, she had allowed herself again to hope and dream that her frustrated musical ambitions would be realized by her son.

As Jerome told her of his new goal, her lips drooped and her eyes contracted with pain. Once again the world of her dreams was crumbling.

"No, not *that* kind of music, Jerry," she exclaimed with shock, after Kern had played for her a few of the

27

songs he had written in London. "That's not for you. That's only for tired and disillusioned hacks. You have talent, real talent. I know."

"Maybe I have talent, Ma," Jerome answered, "but not the kind it takes to write important symphonies and great operas. I've tried, Ma, I really have. But I just haven't got it in me."

"But you're too young to be discouraged, too young to accept defeat," she exclaimed.

Jerome answered firmly, "It's not defeat, Ma, but victory. At last, I've found what I really want to do, to write original and perhaps good music in the only way I can. Maybe I'll never amount to much even as a popular composer. Maybe I'll only become a hack like all the others. But at least I'll bring to my work the enthusiasm and excitement I can't muster for the more serious kind of music."

There was a moment of silence.

Jerome continued eagerly, "I can promise you one thing, Ma. I'll do everything I can to become a *good* composer, even if necessary at the sacrifice of being a *successful* one."

"Very well, Jerry, if that's what you want," she said softly and with a heroic effort at resignation. And she walked away.

CHAPTER FOUR

Songs for Sale

H E MEANT what he had said to his mother: his ambition was to become a *good* composer of popular music rather than a successful one. To become a good composer he knew he would have to learn everything he could about the song business from the ground up—and in the only conservatory where this lesson could be learned, Tin Pan Alley. He therefore went there in search of a job. He soon found one: as a song plugger for the Lyceum Publishing Company, at a salary of seven dollars a week.

It was at just about this time that the song industry had acquired the picturesque name of Tin Pan Alley. The credit for coining the name is now generally given to a journalist named Monroe H. Rosenfeld (who, in his spare time, was also a song-writer). The story goes that in 1903 Rosenfeld was preparing an article on popular music for the New York *Herald*. In search of fresh material, he wandered among the song-publishing houses in New York. At the offices of Harry von Tilzer he came upon an upright piano into which Von Tilzer had stuffed strips of paper through the strings to make it sound like a guitar. Listening to this piano—with its flat, panny sounds—Rosenfeld thought of tin pans. He subsequently called his article "Tin Pan Alley" and thereby christened the entire song business.

At the time the name was coined by Rosenfeld, the song industry was not in an alley but in a street; and the street was 28th Street between Fifth and Sixth Avenues. In the 1890's, two of America's leading song publishers came to 28th Street to set up shop: Remick from Detroit, and Broder and Schlam from San Francisco. This marked the beginning of a general migration of publishers from different parts of New York City to 28th Street: where their formidable competitors were, there the others wished to be too.

Before long, 28th Street began to quiver with the raucous strains of music-making. Next door to Broder and Schlam came Charles K. Harris, who had already become nationally famous with the ballad, "After the Ball," and was now equally prosperous as a publisher. A few doors away from Harris there could now be found Witmark & Sons, a house that had been built on the substantial foundation of a phenomenal song hit: "The Picture That Is Turned to the Wall." A few steps away waved the banners of Harry von

Tilzer advertising his sensational "My Old New Hampshire Home." In the same street were also the house of Joseph Stern (publishers of "Sweet Rosie O'Grady") and that of Leo Feist (then a comparative novice), together with numerous smaller publishers operating on the traditional shoestring, their first successes still to be written. This, then, was a street of song. All day long the pianos banged, the singers warbled, and the feet of tap dancers clicked rhythmically, as new songs were tried out by potential clients.

Although the name of Tin Pan Alley referred specifically to 28th Street, the song industry originated some years earlier (in the 1880's and 1890's) in another section of the city.

Years before it had come uptown, the song business was concentrated on 14th Street between Union Square and Second Avenue. (Before this there had been no geographical concentration of song publishers. They had been scattered throughout the country, found in New York, Chicago, Pittsburgh, Detroit, San Francisco, etc.) There where flourished burlesque theaters, cheap dance halls, saloons, and garden restaurants—together with grand opera at the Academy of Music and the best in variety at Tony Pastor's—popular songs first achieved the status of a major business. There rose in Union Square novice publishers like Stern and Marks, the Witmarks, Shapiro and Bernstein, Charles K. Harris, who entered the publishing business with little more than soaring ambitions and a prayer. They had a desk and they had some songs. They had one thing more: initiative. They sensed that the old methods of promoting songs, which left success to chance, were obsolete. They believed that a song could not only be manufactured like any other commodity but could also be sold to a public like any other commodity.

Formulas for different kinds of songs were set and established in Union Square. There was the sentimental ballad with which the entire decade of 1890 was henceforth to be identified: "My Mother Was a Lady," "The Lost Child," and "After the Ball." There were songs like "My Gal's a Highborn Lady" which evolved from the tunes of the minstrel show and which were soon to inspire ragtime and cakewalk music. There were dialect songs like "Are You the O'Reilly?" and "Down Went McCloskey" in which the swelling migration of Europeans into this country found an echo. There were humorous ditties such as "O Fred, Tell Them to Stop" which were written as specialties for variety shows. So inflexible were the formulas that it was possible for the troubadours of Union Square to write songs without learning how to read or write a note of music; and they could write these songs in wholesale quantities.

More than the technique of song-writing was developed in Union Square. There they discovered the science of song distribution. Once written, songs passed on to the great man of the song industry: the plugger. It was his task to get the songs heard. Upon his charm, salesmanship, personal appearance, contacts, rested the ultimate fate of each song. The plugger had to convince theater managers, orchestra leaders, stars of variety and musical comedy, singing waiters, etc.—anybody who could bring a song to an audience—to use his latest product.

Methods of song plugging varied. One of these originated in 1893. Gus Edwards, later a famous star of vaudeville, but only twelve years old in 1893, scored a sensation when, as part of a vaudeville routine, he repeated a song refrain not on the stage but from a seat in the balcony of the Hurtig and Seamon Theatre in New York. That gave publishers the inspiration for planting singers of their own in theater balconies. When a song had been introduced on the stage, the plugger would suddenly rise in his seat (as if spontaneously), the limelight flashed upon him; and he would repeat the refrain of a song as long as the audience was patient.

A second effective plugging method was evolved a year later by an electrician named George H. Thomas. He produced a series of motion-picture slides which would photographically tell the story of a song. A motion-picture audience was then able to learn a new song and enjoy a community songfest. First used to popularize "A Lost Child," the song slide became an accepted form of entertainment in motion-picture theaters.

When the song business moved from Union Square to Tin Pan Alley, it brought with it its effective system for writing and popularizing songs. But, on 28th Street, the system was developed even further. Song pluggers now went into restaurants, music and department stores, and even on street corners—wherever an audience could be found that would listen to them. Tin Pan Alley could now establish song styles overnight; create stars of the theater; even set into motion new social trends. And it could produce hits with unprecedented fertility. The first decade of the twentieth century was ushered in with "A Bird in a Gilded Cage," (two million copies of sheet music sold) and closed with "Let Me Call You Sweetheart" (five million copies!). During this decade almost a hundred songs achieved a million-copy sale.

Among the great men in Tin Pan Alley when Kern first made his bow there were the sentimental balladist Paul Dresser (brother of the famous American novelist, Theodore Dreiser); the composer-publisher, Harry von Tilzer; the Irish-born composer of lovable operettas, Victor Herbert; and the Broadway song-and-dance man, George M. Cohan. In 1905 the outstanding hits included one of Dresser's finest songs, "My Gal Sal," Victor Herbert's "Kiss Me Again" from the operetta *Mademoiselle Modiste,* Harry von Tilzer's "Wait Till the Sun Shines, Nellie," and George M. Cohan's "So Long, Mary" and "Mary's a Grand Old Name" from his great Broadway success, *45 Minutes from Broadway.*

=======================================

CHAPTER FIVE

The First Shows

KERN was learning the song business. He held various jobs and with several different small publishing houses. Sometimes he played the latest songs of his publishers in a song plugger's cubicle for musicians and performers coming to find some new music; sometimes he wrote stock items for the current song lists. He adapted foreign songs for the American market, made new arrangements of old songs, edited the pieces of illiterate composers. One of his more important jobs was to visit daily the large department stores and the larger music stores of the city. For several hours he would plug his publisher's latest tunes at the piano for prospective sheet-music buyers. In this last assignment he assisted two major figures in Tin Pan Alley. One was Ernest R. Ball who had recently written one of the most famous ballads of the period, "Love Me and the World

Is Mine." The other was an equally successful composer, Jean Schwartz, who was already famous for such hits as "Bedelia" and "Chinatown, My Chinatown."

No assignment was too humble, no work too pedestrian, for Kern. After all, as he often told himself, you cannot begin playing a Beethoven sonata before working slavishly with dull scales. The routine jobs often given him he regarded as the scales which would develop his technique.

Among the hacks of Tin Pan Alley he shone like gold among counterfeit coins. A trained musician was a rare individual in Tin Pan Alley in those days. Kern, who could play the piano fluently, who could read and write music with facility, and who even felt at home in harmony and counterpoint, did not fail to attract notice. Whenever there was a musical assignment that lay beyond the limited powers of the ordinary Tin Pan Alley employee, Kern was called to do the job. And whatever assignment he was given was fulfilled with a quiet and undemonstrative competence that elicited admiration.

He was unusual in another way, too. In an industry filled with brash and cocksure young men given to self-praise, he stood out in contrast. He was quiet and shy, accepting what he knew and what he could do modestly; and he was never heard to publicize himself. He was always ready and eager to give the best that was in him whether he liked what he was doing or not.

He never lost sight of his final goal: to write songs,

36

good songs. We have already noted that his first published song, written while he was still in England,
appeared in 1905: "How'd You Like to Spoon with
Me." (At this same time, the house of E. B. Marks
issued a piano piece of his called "At the Casino.")
He kept on writing songs all the time and persevered
in trying to get them published.

One day, with the quiet confidence and inexperience
of his youth, he walked into the offices of the Harms
Publishing Company for the purpose of seeing and
consulting one of its executives, Max Dreyfus. Dreyfus,
then as now, was one of the most powerful figures in
Tin Pan Alley. Under Kern's arm was a batch of manuscripts. Because Dreyfus was never the man to close his
door to anyone, Kern managed to get an appointment.

Dreyfus' life had been lived in the song business. He
entered it as a boy when Tin Pan Alley was still at
Union Square. His first job was as an errand boy for
the publishing house of Howley and Haviland. Ambitious and resourceful, he worked his way up: shipping
clerk, pianist, arranger, and then minor executive. At
Howley and Haviland, Dreyfus made the first of his
many major song discoveries. He accepted for publication a sentimental ballad called "Just Tell Her That
You Saw Me." The song sold a million copies and the
phrase "just tell her that you saw me" entered into every-
day jargon. This song was the first great hit of one of
the most successful ballad composers of the 1890's,
Paul Dresser.

Dreyfus left Howley and Haviland to join the company of T. B. Harms, then in its infancy. He worked primarily as an arranger, but he filled other spots as well. He plugged songs; he wrote a few under a pseudonym. He also kept a strict watch on the young composers who strayed into his office. Thus he launched and established the career of more than one successful composer. In 1911 he was responsible for giving a major assignment to an obscure young composer. The assignment was to write a score for an operetta called *The Firefly,* and the unknown composer was Rudolf Friml.

Max Dreyfus could not realize it at that time, but when young Jerome Kern timidly entered his office, with a bundle of unpublished songs under his arm, Dreyfus was on the eve of making one of the most important discoveries of his entire publishing history. That was to come later—just as to a later day belongs Dreyfus' discovery of such gifted young composers as George Gershwin, Vincent Youmans, and Richard Rodgers.

Dreyfus looked at the songs Kern brought him and smiled tolerantly.

"Not bad, not bad at all," Dreyfus said as Kern's hopes soared. A moment later those hopes were punctured, for Dreyfus added quickly, "But they're not very good, either."

Then Dreyfus went on to explain. "You are young and inexperienced, and there is much you have to learn. But there is also something in these songs, a vitality and freshness, that is worth nursing. And I'd like to help you."

Dreyfus did not accept any of the songs for publication. Instead, he offered Kern a position as salesman.

"A salesman," he explained, "soon learns from actual experience what kind of song spells success. You will keep a finger on the pulse of the business. I guess there's no better education for a popular composer." Dreyfus then smiled warmly and added, "Besides, if you work for me, I'll be able to keep my eye on you."

As a salesman for the house of Harms—for Kern did not hesitate to accept Dreyfus' offer—he kept on writing songs, and he showed Dreyfus everything he wrote. Before long, Dreyfus accepted a few. Then, increasingly aware of Kern's potentialities, Dreyfus started to use his far-reaching influence to advance the young composer's career. Marie Dressler, later a famous character actress of the movies but at that time a popular vaudevillian, needed a piano accompanist. Kern got the job. He even wrote a song or two for her. Later on, Kern also played the piano for the actress Edna Wallace Hopper, who gave Sunday recitals of popular songs.

There were other assignments closer to Kern's heart. He was asked to contribute songs to various Broadway shows. In 1906, five of his songs were interpolated in *The Rich Mr. Hoggenheimer*, starring Sam Bernard; in 1907 he had five songs in a Julia Sanderson musical, *The Dairy Maid*. Even famous operettas and revivals called to him for songs. He contributed two to Oscar

39

Straus' *The Waltz Dream,* two others for Leo Fall's *The Dollar Princess,* and still another for a revival of *Peter Pan,* starring Maud Adams.

In 1910 Kern received his most important Broadway assignment up to that time. He was asked to rewrite the entire score of a New York show called *Mr. Wix of Wickham.* He revamped the music completely, bringing to the old melodies a daring use of harmony and an original feeling for orchestral color, at the same time contributing several new melodies of his own. The result was music of such originality and freshness that one of the best-known critics in New York, Alan Dale, inquired in his review, "Who is this Jerome Kern whose music towers in an Eiffel way above the average primitive hurdy-gurdy accompaniment of the present-day musical comedy?"

==

CHAPTER SIX

Success

KERN did not have to wait long for success. Hardly had he made his bow on Broadway when he became one of its most prolific and sought-after composers.

One year after *Mr. Wix of Wickham,* he received an important assignment from the well-known producers, the Shuberts. They were opening a new theater in New York, the Winter Garden, to glorify both musical extravaganzas and artistic productions. One of the two opening attractions was an extravaganza called *La Belle Paree,* one of the performers being a young singer subsequently to become one of the greatest attractions of the Winter Garden, Al Jolson. The more serious partner on the same bill was a new Chinese opera, *Bow Sing.* The Shuberts asked Kern to collaborate with another Tin Pan Alley composer, Frank Tours, in writing the music for *La Belle Paree.*

41

The Winter Garden opened on March 20, 1911. That it was opened with a Kern musical was an auspicious beginning for a theater dedicated to revues and musicals; and it marked a major step upward in Kern's career.

From now on the producers began calling on Kern with increasing frequency. In the same year of *La Belle Paree,* Kern's songs were heard in no less than four Broadway productions: *Little Miss Fix It,* starring Nora Bayes and Jack Norworth; *The Hen-Pecks* with Lew Fields; *The Siren* with Julia Sanderson and Donald Brian; and *The Kiss Waltz.* In 1912 came Kern's first complete score for a Broadway show. It was *The Red Petticoat.* This musical was not a success, but its songs were noticed and praised, the best of which included "She's My Girl" and "The Joy of That Kiss." In this same year, George M. Cohan asked Kern to contribute four songs for his production, *A Polish Wedding,* while four other Broadway presentations had Kern songs in them. And in 1913 Kern did the entire score for *Oh I Say* and contributed songs to five other shows.

All this while Kern was gathering his strength for what was to be his most important score and greatest success up to that time. In 1914 he was contracted to write a few songs for a musical by Sydney Jones and Paul Rubens imported from London, *The Girl from Utah.* Like so many other musicals of that period, *The Girl from Utah* (which opened at the Knickerbocker Theatre on December 24, 1914) would have been forgotten long ago, were it not for the fact that for it Kern wrote the first of his great songs. It was a tender tune called "They Didn't Believe Me" (lyrics by Herbert Reynolds), poignantly sung by Julia Sanderson, who played the principal role of a Mormon girl in London. Kern wrote two other fine songs for that show: "You're Here and I'm Here" and "I'd Like to Wander." But "They Didn't Believe Me" was the masterpiece of that score, and the first song by which he will always be remembered. It was also the first of his songs to become a phenomenal nation-wide hit, selling more than two million copies.

One day, soon after the opening of *The Girl from Utah*, Kern played for Victor Herbert the best tunes from that show at the Harms offices. The rotund, genial Irishman, who was then the greatest musical figure in the American theater, listened attentively. "Play that song again," he asked when Kern had gone through "They Didn't Believe Me." When Kern finished, Herbert put his arm around the young composer's shoulders and said, "This man will inherit my mantle."

It was a prophetic remark. It has been proved that nobody but Jerome Kern can honestly be regarded as Victor Herbert's successor. What is particularly interesting is that the prophecy should have been realized so quickly. There was no season now that did not have two, sometimes even three, Kern musicals, not to mention other shows with some Kern songs in them. Within the two-year period of 1917 and 1918, Kern wrote the music for nine musical productions, while between 1915 and 1918 there were nineteen productions on Broadway in which Kern's songs could be heard!

Early in 1915, Broadway saw a show called *90 in the Shade*. It was not very good, and it was not very successful. But in Kern's life story it represents a milestone. It was the first of the Kern musicals for which Guy Bolton wrote the book and lyrics (in this case in collaboration with Clare Kummer). Guy Bolton, who was of English birth, was two years younger than Kern. He was still a novice in the theater, having had his first show presented on Broadway in 1914. And he did not hit his stride as a playwright and lyricist until he joined up with the composer. Together they worked on numerous musical comedies through the years, many of which were outstandingly popular. Some were even significant in changing the course of the American musical theater; for it was not long before Bolton and Kern started evolving a new kind of musical comedy.

Up to now the emphasis had been on extravaganzas: elaborate stage sets, large casts, impressive spectacles. In 1915 Guy Bolton (in collaboration with Paul Rubens) wrote the book and lyrics for a different kind of show, and Kern created the music. It was called *Nobody Home* and was presented at the Princess Theatre. Everything in this show was on a modest scale, a striking contrast to what was then being seen on Broadway. The sets were economical and called for few changes; the casts were small; the production was inti-

44

mate. Even the theater in which it was presented was a miniature.

Nobody Home was a tremendous success. Its producer, F. Ray Comstock, could draw only a single conclusion: audiences were tired of mammoth productions and preferred more credibility and subtlety in their musical plays. He decided to continue presenting little musicals at the Princess Theatre and he asked Bolton and Kern to write a new play in the style of *Nobody Home.*

With the assistance of Philip Bartholomae and Schuyler Green (who helped out with the book) they came up with their first triumph: *Very Good, Eddie.* Everything about this musical was in an intimate and informal vein. There were only twelve girls in the cast; there was very little dancing; there was only a handful of musicians in the orchestra pit; and the costumes and scenery were the last word in simplicity. The singing and acting were both so informal that when Oscar Shaw sang a song or Ernest Truex went through one of his humorous routines, the audience felt that the performance was taking place in its own living room. Some of the critics, accustomed to more ambitious productions, referred to it derisively as "kitchenette production" or as "parlor entertainment." But the audiences loved it. When they left the theater they were humming such singable Kern tunes as "Babes in Woods," "Nodding Roses," "I've Got to Dance," and "Old Bill Baker" (the last with lyrics by Ring Lardner). *Very Good, Eddie* was one of Broadway's most resounding hits of the middle 1910's, running for 341 performances in New York before continuing on the road for another year. It popularized a new *genre* on the American musical-comedy stage (first introduced with *Nobody Home*), a *genre* henceforth known as the "Princess Theatre Shows" after the theater in which they were seen.

On the opening night of *Very Good, Eddie,* Kern found an old friend in the back of the theater, P. G. Wodehouse, who had worked with him in the Frohman office in London. Wodehouse was now an established writer, having achieved success in 1910 with *Psmith in the City* and followed it up with *Psmith, Journalist.* After warm greetings had been exchanged, both recalled nostalgically the days, a decade back, when Wodehouse had written a few lyrics for Kern's first songs.

"We made a pact in those days," Wodehouse reminded Kern. "We said we'd continue our collaboration when both of us became famous."

Kern answered, "I'm willing to stick to the bargain if you are."

Then and there they reached the decision to work together again as soon as possible. The first opportunity arrived in 1916, with the latest of the Bolton-Kern musicals, *Have a Heart.* With Wodehouse serving as the lyricist for Kern's songs and Bolton writing the book, a great triumvirate of the American musical theater came into being; that triumvirate was to be responsible for some of the finest and most successful musical comedies of that era. The three men brought into the musical theater a sparkle and gaiety, a sophistication and wit, a nostalgia and wistfulness it had not known till them.

Many years later Guy Bolton recalled, "We enjoyed our work together. We planned shows, some of them were written, some went the way of dreams. Those were the days of the gay Kern—Kern at thirty—and the Wodehouse gaiety matched his."

Bolton went on to give a portrait of Kern in those days:

> I moved out to Bronxville and lived with Jerry and his wife. . . . My chief trouble with him in Bronxville was that he would never go to bed, and in the middle of the night his puckish fancy would frequently take us off on all-night drives—to arrive surprisingly on the doorstep of some friend in the early hours of morning. Once, when our welcome was a bit forced, Jerry insisted on getting back in the car, announcing that we had dropped in for a five-minute chat. Fortunately, the host and hostess were roused to an effort at hospitality that calmed my friend's ruffled feelings. But we paid no more informal visits to that couple.

CHAPTER SEVEN

A Great Deal of Luck

KERN used to tell interviewers that he was a fellow with "a little bit of talent" and "a great deal of luck."

With his customary modesty he was underestimating his talent. But he was not exaggerating the role luck played in his life. From his boyhood on, he traveled under a favorable star which usually dictated that he be at the right place, or do the right thing, at the right time.

He had been lucky when he had made that unfortunate deal with the pianos, but for which he might have become a businessman instead of a composer. He had been lucky in finding a job as composer of theatrical bits in the Frohman office in London, which directed him toward the writing of popular songs. He had been lucky in finding a young man named Wodehouse in that

49

office, a meeting which was later to bring him one of his most brilliant collaborators.

His luck continued. He was fortunate in the way he found the woman he married. The story of their meeting began on an evening in 1910. Kern was visiting London at that time, and while in his room late one evening a new melody came to him. He wrote it down on paper, then felt an irresistible urge to try it out on a piano. Unfortunately there was none in the room; he would simply have to wait until the morning. Just then the sound of piano-playing came from the adjoining apartment. The impulse to try out his song was so great that he was able to overcome his natural timidity. He knocked at the door of his neighbor. When an attractive girl with soft eyes and gentle smile opened the door for him, he apologized quickly for his intrusion and for his presumptuousness in making a strange request, at that strange hour, for the use of her piano. He explained his problem.

"Of course, of course," she said, her eyes lighting up with laughter. "You see, I understand musicians. I'm a musician myself."

This was the way Kern met Eva Leale. Their friendship developed from that night on and grew into love. They were married on October 25, 1910. And so it had been coincidence and accident (luck is the better word) that brought Kern the woman with whom he was to live happily for almost forty years, up to end of his life.

His lucky star was also at work on a certain fateful night in 1915.

Kern had made arrangements with Charles Frohman to travel to England. Europe was then at war (World War I), and bookings on transatlantic liners out of New York were hard to get. Kern, however, had some pressing business to attend to which demanded his personal attendance in London. He appealed to Frohman, who used his influence to get Kern a booking on the same boat on which he himself was sailing.

On the evening of the midnight sailing, Kern felt unusually tired. He decided to take a brief nap before leaving for the pier, and set his alarm clock to awaken him at the proper time. The clock failed to go off. Kern slept right through the night and missed his boat. Awaking in the morning, Kern cursed himself, his stupidity, his negligence, and above everything else his tough luck. He would now be unable to go to London at all.

But that alarm clock which had failed to go off (and for the first time since Kern had bought it!) had saved his life. For the boat he had missed was the ill-fated *Lusitania*, torpedoed by a German submarine off the Irish coast on May 7, 1915. All those who sailed on it perished, including Kern's friend and first employer, Charles K. Frohman.

Later on in life, Kern's luck still held good. By the time he became a famous and wealthy composer he acquired a mania for collecting rare books and first editions. Once he saw a precious item, the disease for ownership was such that the infection made him uniquely vulnerable. He never had the heart to bargain with a bookseller, and often paid an exorbitant price for the book. For years the word spread in the rare-book business that a full-grown "sucker" had arisen ready to pay any price that was asked of him. Behind Kern's back, the booksellers laughed at his sweet and expensive innocence. It was quite true that Kern paid a higher price than others would have for similar items; but he had luck. During the prosperous years of the late 1920's the rare-book business boomed.

By 1928 Kern's collection, worth a fortune, had become an onerous responsibility robbing him of peace of mind. It included many choice and treasurable items: the only manuscript page in existence of Samuel Johnson's *Dictionary*; the longest available manuscript in hand, a novel by Oliver Goldsmith; a dedication copy of Stevenson's *A Child's Garden of Verses*; the first fourteen chapters, in manuscript, of Thomas Hardy's *A Pair of Blue Eyes*; first editions of poetical works by Keats, Shelley, and Coleridge; the original manuscript of Tennyson's *Maud*; and many, many other precious manuscripts and editions.

Kern suddenly decided to auction off this valuable collection. The same booksellers who had once regarded him as a "sucker" now scrambled over one another in a mad rush to buy back the same books once sold him—

and at far higher prices. A first edition of Robert Burns' poems, for example, which had been valued at $2,000 and which a shrewd bookseller had disposed of to Kern for $6,500 now brought in $23,000! Kern's collection was sold for the aggregate sum of $1,729,000—or almost twice as much as he had paid for it! And as if this profit were not enough, there was an additional and fortunate development. This auction took place only a year before the economic holocaust of 1929 devastated the book market to a point where the Kern collection would have been disposed of at a disastrous loss, if it could have been disposed of at all.

One day after the auction was over, a friend met Kern and asked him, "Now that you sold your collection, Jerry, what hobby are you going to take up?"

Kern smiled and pointed to a slim package under his arm.

"The same one, old man. I guess I'll just have to go ahead and start a new collection. You see, I just found a perfectly wonderful edition, dirt cheap, and I couldn't resist the temptation of buying it."

With the same impetuousness that made him sell his books, Kern one day decided to abandon the stock market because he had suddenly become bored with trading, gambling on commodities, and with following the rise and fall of stock quotations. He had acquired a fortune in securities and he got rid of all of them at the highest possible prices.

Only a few months later came the stock market crash of 1929.

CHAPTER EIGHT

And a Great Deal of Talent

KERN was also lucky in his career, lucky that he had a powerful publisher like Max Dreyfus to help him along toward success, lucky too that he first emerged on Broadway at a time when composers of his talent and background were yet so few and far between. But for such circumstances it is hardly likely that he would have become one of Broadway's most successful composers when he was only twenty-six.

But he also had a great deal of talent. And it was talent, and not luck, that kept him in a position of first importance in American popular music for a generation.

He wrote scores for musical comedies as effortlessly as others write letters—producing not one but several each year. Not all of them were successes, nor were all of equal quality. But they all demonstrated that he was an amazingly facile composer who could be counted on to find the catchy phrase, the lilting tune, the *mot juste* in whatever song he was writing. They also demonstrated that, despite his facility, he never lost the capacity to take pains with his work. His best shows were among the most important in their respective seasons; and his best songs made American musical history.

The great number of Kern musicals makes it difficult to keep track of all of them, and even were this done it is doubtful if the result would justify the effort. The complete list of Kern's musicals represents a boring parade of many now-forgotten names, only a scattered handful of which has any meaning for us today. But a cursory glance at a few of these shows might be illuminating in giving measure to Kern's rapidly growing stature.

In 1916 Kern provided four songs for the *Ziegfeld Follies*. This was a nosegay in Kern's bouquet since Florenz Ziegfeld drew only the cream of the crop in preparing his revues; the cast of the 1916 edition of the *Follies*, for example, included W. C. Fields, Fanny Brice, Ina Claire, and Marion Davies. Ziegfeld's call to Kern emphasizes the high station that the composer was already occupying in Tin Pan Alley. And Ziegfeld was to call on Kern twice more for songs, for his *Follies* of 1917 and 1921.

The year of 1917 saw three Kern-Wodehouse-Bolton collaborations. *Miss 1917* was the most interesting of these because of its extravagant wealth of theatrical talent. The cast included Lilyan Tashman, Van and

Schenck, Lew Fields, and Vivienne Segal—all of them then, or later, among the great names on Broadway. The dancers included at least three of the most remarkable performers of that generation: Ann Pennington, Irene Castle, and George White. In the chorus line was Peggy Hopkins Joyce. Joseph Urban did the sets; Lady Duff Gordon designed the costumes; Adolf Bolm prepared the choreography. (It might be added that the rehearsal pianist for the show was a young fellow named George Gershwin!) All this—and music by Kern, the book by Bolton, and lyrics by P. G. Wodehouse! It would be difficult to find another musical to match this for such riches. Yet *Miss 1917* was a failure and lasted on Broadway only a single month.

But the two other Kern-Wodehouse-Bolton productions, in 1917, met happier fates. *Oh Boy* was an immense success—perhaps because it returned to the charm and intimacy of the "Princess Theatre Shows"; perhaps because it had such wonderful tunes as "Magic Melody" and "Till the Clouds Roll By." *Leave It to Jane,* based on George Ade's *The College Widow,* followed the more conventional pattern of the musical comedy. It, too, was a great success; and it, too, had some memorable songs, principally the "Siren's Song" and "The Sun Shines Brighter."

There were two more popular Kern-Wodehouse-Bolton productions in 1918—*Oh Lady, Lady* and *Oh My Dear.* The next two years brought other shows and other successes, climaxed in 1920 by one of the greatest

57

and most famous of all Kern musicals, *Sally*, presented by Florenz Ziegfeld at the New Amsterdam Theatre on December 21, 1920. Guy Bolton's book and lyrics by Clifford Grey and Buddy DeSylva were serviceable but by no means exceptional. The sweet and sentimental play concerned a dish-washing waif named Sally who invades the houses of the rich where she meets and captures the heart of Blair Farquar of the Social Register. What distinguished *Sally*, what set it sharply apart from the other musicals of the day, were two things. The first was the vivacious and glamorous star, Marilyn Miller. Once described as a "Degas figure turned American," Marilyn Miller was diminutive in size and small of voice; but when she was on the stage she dominated it completely. The other outstanding feature of the show was Kern's score of delectable melodies. When Marilyn Miller (as Sally) and Irving Fisher (as Blair Farquar) sang the poignant duet in the first act, "Look for the Silver Lining," they stopped the show each night. That song is now a Kern classic. (Kern liked the melody so much that the following year he included it in still another musical, *Good Morning Dearie*.) But there were other Kern delicacies in that score too: two other duets sung by Sally and Blair, "Joan of Arc" and "A Wild, Wild Rose," the delightful "Butterfly Ballet" in the third act, and the title song sung by the male chorus.

Two other musicals, in 1920, profited by Kern's music: *The Night Boat* and *Hitchy-Koo of 1920* (the latter with a young and still obscure young singer in the

cast, later to become world-famous as prima donna—
Grace Moore). *Good Morning Dearie,* in 1921, borrowed "Look for the Silver Lining" from *Sally,* as we
have already remarked. But it had a hit of its own in
"Kalua," which, incidentally, brought Kern into the
law courts. For "Kalua" exploited a recurrent boogie-
woogie-like bass then popularized by Fred Fisher in a
song called "Dardanella." Fisher sued Kern for plagiariz-
ing what he regarded as his musical device. The courts
awarded Fisher $250 in damages and a certain amount
of personal satisfaction.

In 1923 there was *Stepping Stones,* appropriately
named, for the cast was headed by the veteran trouper,
Fred Stone, and included his wife Allene and his daughter Dorothy. In 1924, there were two Kern shows:
Sitting Pretty (a huge success) and *Dear Sir* (a failure).
And in 1925 came *Sunny,* tailor-made for Marilyn Miller in an effort to repeat the success of *Sally.* This time
the heroine was a bareback rider in a circus instead of a
dish-washing waif; and this time her great love duet
was "Who?" sung with Paul Frawley. *Sunny* repeated
the far-reaching success of its predecessor both in New
York and in London.

Sunny represents a particularly important event for
the Kern biographer. It brought Kern into partnership
with two writers with whom he was soon to scale the
heights as a composer for the theater. One of them was
Otto Harbach, who wrote the book. Harbach had for
six years been professor of English at Whitman College

in Walla Walla, Washington, and for several years more a newspaper writer and advertising executive in New York, before he invaded the theater. In 1907, a musical called *The Three Twins* used his lyrics, and in 1909 he had his first serious play, *Madame Sherry,* produced on Broadway. Success came to him with his book for one of the most famous operettas of the American theater, *The Firefly,* first seen at the Lyric Theatre in New York on December 2, 1912, its score by Rudolf Friml. By 1925, when he worked with Jerome Kern for the first time, Otto Harbach was one of the great figures in the Broadway theater.

The other writer was a young man named Oscar Hammerstein, 2d, who wrote the lyrics for *Sunny.* The theater was in Hammerstein's blood, and through heredity. His grandfather (after whom he was named) had been the world-famous opera impresario who had founded the Manhattan Opera Company in New York which, in the first years of the twentieth century, was a formidable rival to the Metropolitan Opera. Oscar's father, William, had been the manager of one of New York's greatest vaudeville theaters, the Victoria, and his uncle, Arthur, was one of the most successful producers on Broadway for almost a generation.

Young Hammerstein, studying law at Columbia University and then practicing in New York City for a few months, also had his heart in the theater. His aim was to be a writer for the stage, and as a student in Columbia he had written some sketches for the college shows.

His uncle finally decided to give him a chance to enter the theater, but only on the condition that he try to learn everything he could about the stage before writing another line.

For two years Hammerstein acted as assistant stage manager, making himself generally useful backstage for his uncle's productions. After a few months he was asked to write a lyric for the opening chorus of a musical presented by his uncle. The first lines of his lyric ran as follows:

> *Make yourselves at home*
> *'Neath our spacious dome*
> *Do just as you please*
> *In two and threes, if you'd rather—*
> *But rest assured you'll be no bother.**

It wasn't a very inspired effort, but it marked the official debut of one of the great lyricists of our generation. In 1918, Hammerstein was engaged as stage manager for an Ed Wynn musical, and one year after that for one of his uncle's productions. During this time he wrote a four-act drama, *The Light,* which had an out-of-town tryout in 1919 and which died promptly. In 1920 he wrote his first musical-comedy book, to a score by Herbert Stothart, *Always You,* presented by his uncle at the Central Theatre in New York where it had a run of sixty-six performances. In the same year

* Used by permission of Oscar Hammerstein, 2d.

61

he started collaborating with Otto Harbach, their first show together, *Jimmie,* closing after seventy-one performances, and their second, *Tickle Me,* a moderate success. Hammerstein's first great success came in 1923 with *Wildflower,* in which he collaborated with Otto Harbach in writing the book and lyrics, and the music of which was prepared by Herbert Stothart and Vincent Youmans. This was followed by another triumph: *Rose Marie,* music by Rudolf Friml and Herbert Stothart.

His reputation now established, Hammerstein could work with the most important composers on Broadway. Thus, in 1925, he joined up with the most successful one of them all—Jerome Kern.

Composer and lyricist took to each other immediately, beginning not only a harmonious artistic partnership but also a lifelong friendship. Like Kern, Hammerstein was serious of purpose, cultured, methodical, punctual, devoid of temperament and poses. Like Kern, he had a passion for work and an unceasing determination to do the best job of which he was capable. Both were sparked by an ambition to achieve greatness.

And they were destined to achieve greatness together, with *Show Boat.*

CHAPTER NINE

Show Boat *Is Born*

I T WAS Kern's idea to adapt Edna Ferber's romantic and atmospherically colorful novel, *Show Boat,* to a musical comedy.

For some time now, Kern had been impatient to try something new. He had thus far written numerous musical-comedy scores (he himself would have been at a loss to compute the precise number!) and he was growing increasingly weary of the old formulas. Since the "Princess Theatre Shows" he had done nothing to diverge from the well-beaten paths followed by all the other authors of musical comedies.

On several occasions he had discussed the possibility of changing the musical-comedy structure with some of the leading personalities of the theater. Why not, he argued, bring to musical comedy some of the feeling for atmosphere and local color, some of the insight into

63

characterization, and some of the respect for logical plot construction that distinguish the serious theater? Why not, he argued further, make the musical score an integral, inseparable part of the play (instead of grafting it on artificially), allowing the songs to grow logically out of the action and the characterization? Why not try to produce, he asked eagerly, something basically American, something in which the text and music give voice to our background and culture? Was it impossible, he inquired, to bring artistic dignity to the American musical comedy?

The people he spoke to—dramatists, producers, "angels," other composers—all shook their heads sadly. It just could not be done, they said pessimistically. Audiences came into the musical-comedy theater seeking not stimulation but light entertainment, not novelty but familiar patterns. Besides, the investment involved in the production of a musical comedy was so enormous that "angels" and producers just could not afford to take a chance with anything that had not already been tried and that had not already proved its commercial value.

Kern accepted these arguments and continued working along the familiar lines dictated by tradition. But he was growing increasingly restive with the clichés of his trade.

One day he bought a copy of Ferber's new novel, *Show Boat*, because he had long admired that author and because the title struck his interest. He progressed only halfway through the story when he knew that he had finally found what he had been looking for instinctively for a long time: a suitable subject with which to realize his inmost ambitions for a new kind of musical comedy. A good play—a play from a book like this!—could provide him, he felt, with an additional argument with which to break down the objections of the skeptics.

He reached for the telephone and called his friend, Alexander Woollcott. Hesitantly he asked Woollcott if it were at all possible to meet Edna Ferber personally. Woollcott chuckled at Kern's disarming naïveté in making such a request.

"A chance?" bellowed Woollcott into the telephone. "Not just a chance but a certainty. What you don't seem to realize, my good man, is that Miss Ferber is just as proud to meet Jerome Kern as Jerome Kern is to meet Edna Ferber."

The interview was arranged by Woollcott. During that meeting Kern came straight to the point and explained the principal reason he wanted to see her. He wanted, he said, to make a musical comedy out of *Show Boat*. Would Miss Ferber give him the rights?

Edna Ferber looked quizzically at Kern. He was too deadly serious to be indulging in jest, too sober to have been stimulated by alcohol, too rational to have suddenly gone mad.

"How can you possibly make a musical comedy out of a novel like *Show Boat*?" she asked, bearing in mind all the musical comedies she had seen.

Soberly Kern spoke of his aims for a *new* kind of

65

musical theater which would once and for all part company with the old stilted methods. *Show Boat*, he argued, was the ideal book for this new kind of show.

Edna Ferber said finally, "If you are crazy enough to try it, I guess I'm crazy enough to give you those rights."

Most of Kern's intimate friends and closest collaborators thought him impractical and quixotic in pursuing such a project. They tried to dissuade him from going ahead with it. They insisted, just as Edna Ferber had at first, that *Show Boat* was not musical-comedy material. It did not allow for chorus girls, dance routines, or musical-comedy humor. "*Show Boat* is too arty," they said. "Perhaps you could make it into an opera libretto. But a musical-comedy book—never!"

But *Show Boat* had won Kern over so completely that he would no longer yield to advice or criticism. Quietly, methodically, he went on with his plans. His first job was to convince Oscar Hammerstein, 2d, to go along with him by adapting the novel into a serviceable text. This was comparatively easy, for Hammerstein was also nursing ideals of his own to extend his horizon and to try something really ambitious and new. The next move was for both of them to sell the idea to Florenz Ziegfeld. The gray-haired, practical showman—apostle of the *status quo* in the musical theater—was skeptical about the whole venture and did not hesitate to say so. "It isn't commercial, Jerry, and you know it yourself," he said.

"I'd be a fool to invest a fortune in something I felt I couldn't sell to the public."

Pleas, arguments, promises, eventually wore down the veteran showman to a point where he was more amenable.

"It's just plain suicide for me, Jerry, and probably for you, too," Ziegfeld said at last. "But if that's what you really want to do, and if you feel so strongly about the merit of the undertaking, you can count me in."

Kern and Hammerstein now went to work. The subject seized their imagination and held it enthralled. No other assignment excited them in such a way. "We had fallen in love with it," Hammerstein recalled some years later. "We couldn't keep our hands off it. We acted out scenes together and planned the actual direction. We sang to each other. We had ourselves swooning."

None of Kern's other scores went so easily as this one, even though he had always been facile. Situations in the play, idiosyncrasies of the characters, the backgrounds and moods, were all so stimulating that the melodies came from him naturally. Sometimes his inspiration came from a source other than the play itself. "Ol' Man River"—with which he hoped to project the atmosphere of the play, set as the story was along the banks of the Mississippi—was born in his mind during a reading of Mark Twain's *Life on the Mississippi*. In one case he used old material. He needed a languorous torch song for the character Julie, and he recalled that some years earlier he had written just such a song with P. G. Wodehouse called "Bill"; the song fit the new score as if made to order.

The enthusiasm and excitement of both Kern and Hammerstein infected even Edna Ferber, who all the while had been skeptical about the project. In her autobiography,* Ferber recalled her emotions on hearing the Kern songs for the first time:

> As the writing of the musical play proceeded (and its up and downs were even more heartbreaking than those of most musical plays), I heard bits and pieces of the score. . . . I had heard "Can't Help Lovin' Dat Man" with its love-bemused lyric. I had melted under the bewitching strains of "Make Believe" and "Why Do I Love You" and Gaylord Ravenal's insolent and careless gambler's song. And then Jerome Kern appeared at my apartment late one afternoon with a strange look of quiet exaltation in his eyes. He sat down at the piano. He doesn't play the piano particularly well and his singing voice, though true, is negligible. He played and sang, "Ol' Man River." The music mounted, mounted, and I give you my word my hair stood on end, the tears came to my eyes, and I breathed like a heroine in a melodrama. This was great music. This was music that would outlast Jerome Kern's day and mine. I have never heard it since without the emotional surge.

* *A Peculiar Treasure* (New York: Doubleday, Doran & Co., 1939).

68

CHAPTER TEN

Show Boat *Is Produced*

BEFORE it was finally produced, *Show Boat* went through heartbreaking tribulations. More than once did Florenz Ziegfeld lose heart and come to the authors with the half-apologetic decision that he had decided not to go ahead with the production. He would explain that it was just not *his* kind of theater and that he would not know what to do with it. Each time both Kern and Hammerstein had to start from the very beginning with their arguments, cajolery, and prayers to win him back to their way of thinking.

Ziegfeld finally decided that he would open the show in his new, magnificent Ziegfeld Theatre then being built on Sixth Avenue. However, when the Ziegfeld Theatre was completed and ready to open, *Show Boat* was still in the formative stage, and another Ziegfeld musical, *Rio Rita*, had to take its place. *Rio Rita* was a tremendous box-office success. This only served once again to dampen Ziegfeld's interest in *Show Boat*, to convince him anew that what the public wanted was shows like *Rio Rita* and not some novel experiment.

"Look, fellows," Ziegfeld told Kern and Hammerstein. "I'm still going ahead with *Show Boat* because I promised you I would. But *Rio Rita* is such a smash hit that it's sure to run at least a year, and I'd still like to have *Show Boat* in the Ziegfeld Theatre. How about delaying the opening of *Show Boat* until *Rio Rita* closes? Besides, I'm too tired to start work on a new show just yet."

Show Boat simply had to be delayed for another year or so, to the intense disappointment of its authors, eager to see their dream come to life. But the delay proved providential, as Hammerstein himself disclosed, for it meant that Kern and Hammerstein could do some more work on it. "The delay made *Show Boat* a much better play than it would have been had we produced the first draft."

There were other agonizing trials even when the production was finally ready. The tryout, at the National Theatre in Washington, D. C., on November 15, 1927, revealed that the show was an hour and a half too long. Elaborate cuts had to be made before the show could come to New York—each cut a knife wound in the hearts of the authors. At last, not a single song, not a single line of dialogue could be deleted. Still a half hour too long, *Show Boat* was presented at the Ziegfeld Theatre in New York on December 27, 1927.

If Florenz Ziegfeld had been hesitant and pessimistic about the play up to curtain time, he did not betray his doubts in the quality of his production. He spared neither energy nor expense in mounting the play as handsomely as he could. (He always worked that way, giving of his best and never sparing himself or the budget.) The scenery of Joseph Urban and the costumes of John Harkrider were lavish without sacrificing good taste. Ziegfeld provided a star-studded cast. Charles Winninger was Cap'n Andy; Helen Morgan, Julie; Edna May Oliver, Parthy Ann; Howard Marsh and Norma Terris, Ravenal and Magnolia; Jules Bledsoe, Joe. If *Show Boat* was to be a failure—at least so argued Ziegfeld, who always did things in the grand manner— it would at any rate be a *magnificent* failure; if he was to go down in defeat, he would succumb majestically. . . .

But to the amazement of everybody concerned with it (even the authors themselves) *Show Boat,* far from being a failure, was a triumph. It was, in truth, a wonderful show, every moment of it. When the opening-night audience succumbed to its spell, it was not aware that it was present at the birth of a new epoch in the American theater. The audience was conscious only of the fact that it was getting grand entertainment.

The first-act curtain rose on a levee along the Mississippi River. But the principal action of the first of the two acts took place aboard *Cotton Blossom,* a show boat

71

that plied its way along the river in the 1880's, stopping off at towns large and small along the river banks. This is the picturesque setting for the love affair of the easy-going but lovable gambler, Gaylord Ravenal, and Magnolia, the charming and well-protected daughter of Cap'n Andy, owner of the boat. Since the lovers cannot get the blessings of Cap'n Andy and his wife, they elope and settle in Chicago. There they begin married life, made turbulent through the varying vicissitudes of a gambler's fortunes. At last, though they still love each other deeply, they separate. Magnolia supports herself by singing at the Chicago Fair Midway the songs she had learned on her father's show boat. She is found there unexpectedly by her father, who brings her back to his boat. Eventually Gaylord and Magnolia are reconciled. And their daughter Kim grows up to become a star on the *Cotton Blossom,* in 1927, singing the songs that had been heard in the 1880's.

As this poignant story unfolded, Kern's songs enriched and deepened the beauty and sentiment of the play. First there was the wistful love duet of Ravenal and Magnolia, "Make Believe." After that, came what has since been deservedly accepted as one of the greatest American songs of all time: Joe's hymn to the Mississippi River, "Ol' Man River." "Here is a song," explained Hammerstein, "sung by a character who is a rugged and untutored philosopher. It is a song of resignation with a protest implied." The words and melody had the simplicity and the deep feeling of a Negro spiritual.

After "Ol' Man River," the tender quintet, "Can't

Help Lovin' Dat Man," was heard. The second act brought back these songs and contributed others no less memorable, including "Bill," "Why Do I Love You?" "You Are Love," and "Nobody Else But Me."

After the final curtain the audience rose to cheer. And the following day the critics echoed these cheers. "It is a complete demonstration of the composer's and lyric writer's dependence on their basic idea . . . a fidelity unrecognized by most musical-comedy book makers." So wrote Alison Smith in the New York *World*. "One of the outstanding triumphs of the season," wrote Richard Watts, Jr., in the New York *Herald Tribune*, "a beautiful example of musical comedy." "An American masterpiece," exclaimed Robert Garland in the *Telegram*. And Alan Dale wrote in the *American*: "Here at last we had a story that was not submerged in the trough of musical molasses; here we had a 'book,' the humor of which emerged naturally and the unusual quality of which struck one as something peculiarly different. *Show Boat* is going to have a wonderful sail —no storms—no adverse winds—nothing to keep it from making port—goodness knows when."

Overnight *Show Boat* passed from a reckless gamble into a gilt-edged investment. It was a hit, one of the greatest of that or any other season. It ran in New York for 572 performances, grossing approximately $50,000 at each one. Then the production went on tour: to London, Paris, St. Louis, Louisville, Dallas, Chicago, Detroit, and San Francisco. After that it returned to Broadway for an additional run.

73

:(::(

CHAPTER ELEVEN

Show Boat *Is Immortal*

SHOW BOAT is the greatest musical comedy of the American theater. It was one of the first musical comedies with dramatic truth, genuine characterizations, authentic backgrounds, and sincere emotions. It was one of the first musical productions in which all the elements of the musical theater were so completely integrated that each is indispensable to the artistic whole. *Show Boat* skillfully combined serious and popular elements—so much so that this work, meant primarily for popular consumption, has retained its significance as art. It can be regarded as a folk play with folk music. And it is very possible that some day it may be performed in the opera house.

Because they had the courage to do something new, original, and important—and because they brought to their task excitement and love—both Oscar Hammerstein, 2d, and Jerome Kern uncovered altogether new creative strength and hitherto unsuspected creative resources. Never before had Hammerstein brought to his lyrics such grace and suppleness, a new kind of simple and wistful beauty; never before had his dialogue had such ease and authenticity; never before did his writing possess such force, economy, and inevitability.

But it is the score that is the abiding miracle of *Show Boat*. In *Show Boat*, Kern develops from a highly talented composer into a great one. A much deeper and richer strain enters his musical writing as his lyric line grows more and more original, his changes of modulation more and more daring, his rhythm increasingly varied, and his moods more subtle.

Such music could even attract the praise of a serious music critic. Olin Downes, the music critic of the New York *Times*, wrote: "This is a score which by reason of its melodic inspiration, its workmanship, its reflection of period and environment has . . . won the position of a classic of its kind."

A triumph in 1927, *Show Boat* has since become a staple in the American theater, returning to our stage at periodic intervals to enchant and inspire us anew with each revival. It was performed again in 1930, at the National Theatre in Washington, D.C., with most of the members of the original cast supplemented by such newcomers as Irene Dunne, Maude Ream Stover, and Margaret Carlisle. In 1932 it started a new long run in New York at the Casino Theatre, the cast including many of the original members except for a new Ravenal, Joe, and Queenie (Dennis King, Paul Robeson, and Tess Gardella). The first film version was made in 1929, a Universal picture starring Laura La Plante, Joseph Schildkraut, and Alma Rubens; this was mostly a silent picture with a synchronized score and only a few talking and song sequences. The first all-talking, all-singing motion-picture version came in 1936, once again from the Universal studios, but this time with Allan Jones, Irene Dunne, Helen Morgan, Paul Robeson, and Charles Winninger. (This screen adaptation had two new songs by Kern and Hammerstein, "Ah Still Suits Me" and "I Have the Room Above Her.")

Since then *Show Boat* has often been revived, not only in New York but in many different parts of the country. The 1946 revival, with Jan Clayton, Carol Bruce, Charles Fredericks, and Kenneth Spencer, started a successful run at the place where the show was born, the Ziegfeld Theatre. It then went on a twelve-month tour of the country. Still another motion-picture adaptation (the finest of all) was made in 1951, starring Ava Gardner and including Kathryn Grayson, William Warfield, and Howard Keel.

In 1941 the music of *Show Boat* was heard in a symphonic adaptation made by Kern, called *Scenario* and performed by many of the country's leading orchestras. (*Scenario* is discussed in a later chapter.) In 1952 *Show Boat* was heard in a new concert version, at the

77

Lewisohn Stadium in New York City. For this performance, a special narrative was prepared by Oscar Hammerstein, 2d, to connect the various songs.

John Chapman, the New York drama critic, wrote in 1946 about *Show Boat:* "It proves to be immortal. It is what every musical comedy should be—and no other has been."

The well-known writer and connoisseur of the lively arts, Gilbert Seldes, expressed his admiration for *Show Boat* in another way. In a personal letter to S. L. Rothafel (the well-known motion-picture impresario, better known in his day as "Roxy"), Seldes wrote in 1932: "I think that if you get a *Show Boat* to produce you will be far luckier than if you find another *Madama Butterfly*."

CHAPTER TWELVE

Good-by, Broadway

IN THE early 1930's Kern continued boldly along the new paths blazed for musical comedy by *Show Boat* with two of his greatest successes.

But first there was temporary digression. In 1929 Kern and Hammerstein wrote *Sweet Adeline*. Starring Helen Morgan and Charles Butterworth, it opened at the Hammerstein Theatre on September 3. This was a formal, even stilted, romance of the Gay Nineties which remained true to the old formulas of musical comedy. Though *Sweet Adeline* was given a handsome production by Arthur Hammerstein and contained two fine Kern songs—"Why Was I Born?" and "Here Am I," both poignantly rendered by Helen Morgan—the audiences rejected it.

With his next production, Kern followed the more original lines of *Show Boat* and regained the favor of his public. The play, described by the program as a "musical love story," was written not by Hammerstein but by Otto Harbach. It was called *The Cat and the Fiddle,* and its cast included Odette Myrtil, Bettina Hall, George Meader, and Georges Metaxa. The story centered around the love affair of an American girl crazy about popular music, and a serious Rumanian composer. Love finally created a bond not only between the American and the Rumanian but also between popular and serious music. *The Cat and the Fiddle* was by no means a *Show Boat.* But in comparison to the run-of-the-mill Broadway musicals its plot was original and developed with credibility; and it courageously dispensed with some of the long-accepted paraphernalia of the musical-comedy theater (such as chorus girls). But its greatest single asset was the Kern score, one of his most original. Included such melodic delights as "She Didn't Say Yes" and "The Night Was Made for Love," and at one point was sufficiently ambitious and adventurous to include a neatly constructed fugue. *The Cat and the Fiddle* started its long and successful New York run at the Globe Theatre on October 15, 1931.

There was even greater daring in both the text and the score of *Music in the Air,* with which the Kern-Hammerstein collaboration was resumed. The setting of this "musical adventure" (as the authors called it) was the picturesque Bavarian town of Edendorf. Karl and Sieglinde are in love. But the course of their romance grows complicated when a famous musical-comedy star develops an interest in Karl, while Sieglinde is pursued by a librettist who wants her to appear in his play. Everything, of course, works out well in the end: Karl and Sieglinde return penitently to each other and find happiness together in lovely Edendorf.

It is true that this kind of plot was more or less grist for the typical musical-comedy mill. But Oscar Hammerstein, 2d, brought a fresh treatment to it and filled it with heart-warming charm, *Gemütlichkeit,* and picturesque atmosphere. And once again Kern responded sensitively to a fine text with an outstanding score. The best songs included "I've Told Ev'ry Little Star" (the inspiration for which came to the composer when he heard the chirpings of a New England sparrow), "The Song Is You," and "Egern on Tegern Sea," the last suggesting a Bavarian folk song. Once again, as in *Show Boat,* music and drama were so beautifully integrated that some of the appeal of the score is lost without the stage business.

Music in the Air—with Walter Slezak, Katherine Carrington, Natalie Hall, Tullio Carminati, Reinald Werrenrath, Al Shean, and Marjorie Main!—opened at the Alvin Theatre on November 8, 1932, and ran for 342 performances. After that, it was seen in Boston, New Haven, Newark, Philadelphia, Pittsburgh, and Chicago. It was described by Brooks Atkinson in the New York *Times* as "the emancipation of the musical drama." He went on further to say: "Without falling back into the clichés of the trade, Hammerstein has written sentiment and comedy that are tender and touching. It is an amusing story and an effortless piece of craftsmanship, and it provides a perfect setting for Kern's score." Robert Benchley remarked in *The New Yorker*: "What with laughing and crying, crying and laughing, I had an elegant time."

There was a new Kern musical in 1933 which reverted to type. It was *Roberta,* book by Otto Harbach, based on a story of Alice Duer Miller. *Roberta,* whose setting was a fashionable dress establishment in Paris, was an excuse for a lavish fashion show. It was a somewhat dull and slow-moving play, which would probably have been doomed to failure if it had not been the showcase for one of Kern's most iridescent jewels. When, in the second act, the lovely Tamara sang "Smoke Gets in Your Eyes," she brought down the house. The song spelled success for the entire show. It was one of Kern's finest lyrical inspirations (he regarded this song as his personal favorite) and one of the greatest songs to come out of Tin Pan Alley. Its tremendous popularity threw into the shade two other outstanding songs, both of which have since become popular. One was "Yesterdays," sung by one of the great ladies of the American theater, Fay Templeton, in what was to be her farewell appearance. The other was a duet sung by Tamara and Allan Jones, "The Touch of Your Hand."

It is interesting to note parenthetically that more than a great song was born in *Roberta:* a great Hollywood star. One of the performers in the play was a young, likable, humorous fellow by the name of Bob Hope.

What was destined to be Kern's last Broadway musical —once again in the more formal style—was also one of his failures. It was called *Very Warm for May*, presented at the Alvin Theatre on November 17, 1939, with a fine cast including Donald Brian, Avon Long, Eve Arden, and Jack Whiting. It closed after only fifty-nine performances. This rather attenuated play, about a summer stock company and the tangled love affairs of two young society people with stage-struck children of a veteran from the theater, was, as Brooks Atkinson wrote, "a singularly haphazard invention that throws the whole show out of focus and makes an appreciation of Mr. Kern's music almost a challenge."

Thus Kern brought his incomparable career on Broadway to an anticlimactic end with a box-office failure. But that final bow was not made without the offering of a masterpiece. When Kern wrote his song, "All the Things You Are," for this show, he prophesied that it would never become popular since its subtle enharmonic changes and unorthodox intervallic structure made it "too hard for the public." But he was wrong. "All the Things You Are" not only became very popular; it also became a classic. If *Very Warm for May* is remembered today it is only because it made possible the birth of one of the finest songs written by an American composer.

CHAPTER THIRTEEN

Hello, Hollywood

HOLLYWOOD had adapted *Show Boat* for the first time in 1929, as we have already noted. In the same year, and in 1930, *Sally* and *Sunny* were brought to the screen, both starring Marilyn Miller and both using the songs from the original stage production. In 1930 a Fox film called *Three Sisters* used a new Kern number, "Lonely Feet."

With the further development of the talking picture in the first year or two of the 1930's, and with its acceptance by the public, there was a frenzied need in Hollywood for composers, writers, and performers who could work within the new medium. It was inevitable for the industry to call immediately to Jerome Kern, since he was the leading composer on Broadway. He listened to this call in 1931. For the rest of his life he

85

was to work for Hollywood, and after 1939 he was to work for it exclusively.

His first assignment was to write an original score for a movie called *Men of the Sky*. He was to write many other original scores for the screen after that. In 1935 there was *I Dream Too Much*, with Lily Pons; in 1936 *Swing Time*, with Ginger Rogers and Fred Astaire, one of whose songs, "The Way You Look To-night," winning the award of the Motion Picture Academy; in 1937 *When You're in Love*, with Grace Moore, and *High, Wide and Handsome* (original screenplay by Oscar Hammerstein, 2d), with Irene Dunne; in 1938 *The Joy of Living*, with Irene Dunne and Douglas Fairbanks, Jr.; in 1940 *One Night in the Tropics*, with Allan Jones and Nancy Kelly; and after that, *You Were Never Lovelier* and *Cover Girl*, both with Rita Hayworth; *Can't Help Singing*, with Deanna Durbin; and *Centennial Summer* with Jeanne Crain, Linda Darnell, and Cornel Wilde.

Besides writing these original scores, Kern also helped adapt his most famous Broadway shows for the screen. *The Cat and the Fiddle* was done in 1933 by MGM with a cast including Ramon Navarro, Jeanette MacDonald, Frank Morgan, Charles Butterworth, Jean Hersholt, and Vivienne Segal. One year later Fox presented the screen version of *Music in the Air*, with Gloria Swanson and John Boles. The RKO studios screened *Roberta* in 1935, the star-studded cast including Ginger Rogers, Fred Astaire, Irene Dunne, Ran-

dolph Scott, and Helen Westley. In the same year
Sweet Adeline was produced by Warner Brothers,
starring Irene Dunne. A second movie version of *Show
Boat* came in 1936 and a new screen adaptation of
Sunny in 1941.

It was in Hollywood that Kern met for the first time
the man destined to become one of his leading propa-
gandists and most eloquent musical interpreters: the
orchestral conductor, André Kostelanetz. Kostelanetz
had come to Hollywood with his wife—the celebrated
prima donna of the Metropolitan Opera, Lily Pons—
who was to appear in the Kern screen musical, *I Dream
Too Much*. Kostelanetz had already frequently performed Kern's songs over the radio and on phonograph
records and had an immense respect not only for Kern's
talent but also for his lofty position in the field of
American popular music.

Before he met Kern, Kostelanetz expected to find him,
like so many other successful men he knew, "self-
assured, a little egocentric, given to recitation of recent
successes," in Kostelanetz' own words. But Kern's first
words to Kostelanetz were as startling as his gentle,
dignified, and unassuming manner.

"Really, Mr. Kostelanetz," Kern said quietly, "I'm
embarrassed to write music for a great singer like Miss
Pons. I'm just not worthy of such an honor."

"The way he spoke," Kostelanetz explained, "the
muscles of his face taut, his eyes contracted, you knew

that he was deadly serious, just as you knew, too, that once he got down to work he would do a job that would take your breath away."

Kern did produce several outstanding songs for Lily Pons, songs she enjoyed singing on the screen, and subsequently over the air and on phonograph records. The finest of these were "I Dream Too Much," "Jockey on the Carousel," and "I'm the Echo—You're the Song I Sing."

After their association in *I Dream Too Much* came to an end, Kern and Kostelanetz became good friends. The conductor never forgot the impression Kern had made on him during those first meetings, and he always kept recalling his first surprised impressions of the composer to mutual friends.

CHAPTER FOURTEEN

"Can't Help Lovin' Dat Man"

WITH the center of his activity now in Hollywood, Kern acquired a spacious white brick house on Whittier Drive in Beverly Hills. Here he was to live for the rest of his life with his wife, his daughter Elizabeth Jane (who married and later divorced jazz musician Artie Shaw), and his champion boxer, Sieglinde von Hirschfield (winner of several cups and ribbons at dog shows).

Kern loved that house because it provided him with a glimpse of sky, trees, and flowers, and enabled him to hear all the time the chirping of birds—pleasures usually denied him in the big city. He particularly liked his studio. Almost from the time he moved into the house, the studio gave the impression of hopeless confusion, what with books, music, pictures, curios, knick-knacks, papers, correspondence, scattered about in disorder. Within that studio he found relaxation by reading books or listening to the radio or phonograph (puffing at his pipe as he read or listened). Here he entertained his intimate friends, always insisting on mixing their drinks himself. (He himself partook of alcohol only late in the afternoon, and then allowing himself no more than two cocktails.) Here he did his work, frequently with the radio going full blast.

He was a hard worker. He never waited for inspiration to come before going to the piano and starting composing. He once told an interviewer, "If you wait for inspiration to light on your shoulder and gently poke cobwebs from your brain you had better change your profession. Even if a few hours at the piano do not result in a song hit you will get an idea, a striking combination of notes, a few bars from constant work. And these things are the basis of good songs." Once he started working he was methodical and systematic, spending many consecutive hours at the piano. Hardly a day passed without some new music being written and some old music being revised. "You get a nibble and you don't know whether it is a minnow or a marlin until you reel it in," he explained. "You write twenty tunes to get two good ones, and the wastebasket yearns for the music." That was his method—to keep working all the time at the good and the bad, and to eliminate the chaff from the wheat. ("Lord, how I like to cut!") He used to say good-humoredly that he had an infallible method for determining which was the wheat and which the chaff. When he tried out a song—so he said—he would look at the bust of Wagner on his piano. If the bust smiled, he knew he had written a good song; when it scowled, he recognized a failure. "Another method," he once said with more wit than malice, "is to play it for my wife. If she doesn't like it, I know I have a hit on my hands."

He usually worked at the piano, trying out and changing a melody until it acquired the shape and form that pleased him. Only then would he put the melody down on paper with pen and ink. When a song was finished he would play it into a recording machine (which his daughter would operate for him) and, the recording made, would dispatch it to his lyricist—for, in his case at any rate, the melody always came before the lyric. While working, he would suck at his pipe, interrupting this practice by munching at a piece of candy, a box of which was invariably at hand.

He was a stickler for details, whether he was working on a muscial play, a screenplay, or a song. Oscar Hammerstein noted this fact in the preface to his book, *Lyrics:*

> During my several collaborations with Jerry I absorbed his habit of being painstaking about very small things. I was surprised at first to find him deeply concerned about details which I thought did not matter much when there were so many important problems to solve in connection with writing and producing a play. He proved to me, eventually, that while people may not take any particular notice of any one small effect,

the over-all result of finickiness like his produces a polish which an audience appreciates.

Kern was not a good pianist; as the years passed he kept on deteriorating. He played his own music poorly. His friends used to say that there was always one acid test for a Kern song which, if passed successfully, would prove its true mettle; and the test was Kern's own performance. Once Kern played one of the songs he had just written for a forthcoming motion picture to some Hollywood moguls. When he finished they shook their heads sadly. This song, they were certain, was third-rate Kern. But the song he had played was "The Way You Look Tonight," winner of an Academy award.

As he looked quizzically at you out of his horn-rimmed glasses, and spoke to you with his well-modulated voice, you understood why they sometimes called him "the professor." He not only looked like a professor, but talked like one. His vital interest in and his remarkable fund of knowledge about things cultural never failed to impress those who came into contact with him. However, his dress belonged more to Beverly Hills than to the college campus. He always wore expensive, custom-tailored clothing with charming casualness. The cut was conservative and in the best possible taste. His only excesses were loud-colored ties, a startling contrast to his otherwise sober dress, and occasionally vivid-colored slacks and shirts when he was less formally attired.

"Can't Help Lovin' Dat Man"

He was the easiest man in the world to get along with. He never put on fake attitudes, poses, or fits of temperament. Even when he was in the midst of rehearsing a new show—always an ordeal to try the soul of even a saint—he rarely lost his equilibrium. On those occasions he was energetic, dynamic, indefatigable, critical, methodical, exacting, precise, but rarely brusque or ill-mannered. He could be as courteous to a stagehand or to a scrubwoman who cleaned up after the rehearsals as to one of the stars. Indeed, it was his practice when he wrote a new song while a show was in rehearsal to gather around him some of the humbler characters of the theater and humbly ask for their reaction.

This story of his life has already on several occasions pointed to his modesty and self-effacement. One could spend an entire evening with him without hearing a word about himself or his achievements. He liked talking shop, of course—but when he did it was always about the work of others and never digressed into autobiography. When he praised the achievements of rival composers, which he did often, he was generous and sincere. But when he himself was praised he would grow flustered and brush the praise aside impatiently and change the subject.

He did not have many diversions. He never gambled and he drank very little. Smart parties bored him. He rarely went to night clubs. His entire life was untouched by scandal, or rumor of scandal. Essentially his pleasures were those of simple people—a good book, a good piece of music, a stimulating conversation. "I am really a very dull fellow," he would say of himself. His favorite composers were Wagner, Tchaikovsky, and Irving Berlin. On the rare occasions when he was tempted to speak about his songs he would always single out "Smoke Gets in Your Eyes" as his best.

His only participation in sports was through golf. He started playing as far back as 1905. Thirty-five years after that he succeeded in hitting a hole-in-one. "Now," he remarked wistfully, in commenting on this feat, "nobody wants to play with me." He had a veritable passion for telephoning; in his leisure hours he was usually found at the telephone making calls to friends, even across the country. On the other hand, he considered the writing of letters a chore.

He had an infectious sense of humor. There was the time an actress, who kept rolling her "r's" all the time, said to him, "You want me to cr-r-r-r-r-ross the stage? How can I get acr-r-r-r-r-ross?" "My dear," he answered politely," "why don't you just roll on your r-r-s?"

One winter Kern and Franklin P. Adams (F.P.A.) were driving in Florida. They stopped off at an Indian reservation and began talking to a squaw who explained that she was a Cree, and one of the last to be found in this country. "Ah!" commented Kern, "la dernière Cree!"

CHAPTER FIFTEEN

Jerome Kern—Of Carnegie Hall

HIS fame was growing all the time. Again and again there was testimony to his lofty position in American music. In 1935 Alexander Woollcott—at that time famous as the "Town Crier" over the radio—conducted a birthday party for Kern on his regular network program. Four years later the stage show of the Radio City Music Hall, in New York, featured a cavalcade of Jerome Kern hits—a lavish revue in five scenes drawing its songs from *Good Morning Dearie, Show Boat,* and *Music in the Air.* In 1944 the week of December 11 was designated Jerome Kern Jubilee Week. Paul Whiteman was its chairman. Throughout the country, Kern's music was played over the air, in theaters, night clubs, and ballrooms, as a tribute to the nation's song maestro.

His importance as a composer of popular music was not questioned. But, during the 1930's, some of the most serious musicians in the country were ready to concede that Kern's songs, written in a popular idiom, were good enough to receive serious artistic consideration. Some of the most notable representatives of the concert world—musicians like Lily Pons, John Charles Thomas, Paul Robeson, and many others—now included Kern songs on their serious concert programs, as well as in performances over the air and on records. The Gordon String Quartet, whose repertoire included only the finest examples of string-quartet music from Beethoven to Bartók, played "The Song Is You" and "The Way You Look Tonight" (adapted for string quartet) in several of their concerts and later recorded them. In November, 1936, the Philadelphia Orchestra presented on one of its programs the waltz from *Swing Time* (orchestrated by Robert Russell Bennett).

Two famous orchestral conductors also insisted on taking Kern seriously. Recognizing that he had native talent, taste, originality, and melodic freshness, these two conductors wanted him to turn to forms more expansive than that of the song, and to media more ambitious than that of the voice. In short, they wanted Kern of Tin Pan Alley to make a bid for Carnegie Hall with symphonic works.

In 1941 Artur Rodzinski, then the conductor of the Cleveland Orchestra, asked Kern to write a large symphonic work with the melodies from *Show Boat*. When Kern recovered from his incredulity and shock at being asked to write music for a symphony orchestra, he expressed doubt as to his ability to complete such an assignment. "I just don't belong in Carnegie Hall," he told Artur Rodzinski. But Rodzinski was persistent and broke down Kern's resistance.

Kern spent three months on a score which he called *Scenario,* completing the orchestration in September, 1941. One month later Rodzinski performed *Scenario* in Cleveland with the Cleveland Orchestra, and in December of the same year in New York with the New York Philharmonic-Symphony Orchestra.

"This is the greatest thing that has happened to me," Kern remarked after the Cleveland première.

Scenario was dedicated to Rodzinski. The published score contained the following quotation by Winston Churchill, then the wartime Prime Minister of England:

> The British Empire and the United States . . .
> together . . . I do not view the process with misgiving.
> No one can stop it. Like the Mississippi, it just keeps
> rolling along. Let it roll . . . inexorable, irresistible, to
> broader lands and better days.

Scenario is made up of the best-known melodies from *Show Boat.* "Ol' Man River" is heard first in the violas and clarinets. "Can't Help Lovin' Dat Man" follows in muted trumpet. After some development, we hear "Make Believe" and "Why Do I Love You?" The work ends with an effective recall of "Ol' Man River." But *Scenario* is no mere potpourri or a patchwork quilt. It is an integrated work in which the different melodies are skillfully and naturally fused into a single artistic creation.

"There is a simplicity and directness of procedure in this scenario as sincere, simple, direct as Mr. Kern himself," wrote Olin Downes in the New York *Times*, "and so remote from the sophisticated symphonic craftsmen as to be rather deliciously naïve. But the melodies themselves! . . . At least half a dozen are irresistible and unforgettable. It is a native idiom, and it is excellent melodic invention. It smacks with sheer direct inspiration and without any pose. . . . It is infinitely further towards a native form than the vast majority of our cerebral and imitative American symphonies."

Virgil Thomson also expressed enthusiasm for Kern's wonderful melodies in the *Herald Tribune:*

> It would not be just to fail to state here one's admiration for their graceful and refined construction. . . . They are pleasant to hear . . . in almost any orchestral dress. . . . The cannonade of applause that followed led me to fancy that Dr. Rodzinski has probably presented the musical world with a number that will bring pleasure to countless thousands in pop concerts all over the still civilized world.

Soon after these première performances of *Scenario*—and soon after Pearl Harbor and America's entry into World War II—André Kostelanetz came to Kern with a major orchestral assignment. Inspired by the times,

Kostelanetz decided to commission several important American composers to produce orchestral works on some American subject or on some famous American personality. Aaron Copland was to write for Kostelanetz *A Lincoln Portrait,* and Virgil Thomson the *Mayor La Guardia Waltzes.* Kostelanetz—convinced that Kern belonged in the company of such serious composers— wanted a similar work from him.

Once again Kern was overwhelmed with doubts and self-deprecation. Such a job, he felt, was not for his limited gifts. "Copland—yes!" Kern told Kostelanetz. "But not for me, André! I'm only a fellow from Tin Pan Alley."

But it did not take much persuasion and argument for Kostelanetz to win Kern over—not now that Kern had tried his hand at a serious piece of music and had not made a fool of himself. He accepted the assignment, selecting Mark Twain as a subject, and went to work. "All else is laid aside in my tremendous enthusiasm for the project," he wrote to Kostelanetz before long, "which for the past forty-eight hours or so has made me well-nigh breathless."

Kostelanetz has written how Kern gave himself completely to this task once he had started:

He showered me with letters, giving me details of what he was doing, and why he was doing it. These letters are really priceless in giving us an insight into the workings of a creative mind. Kern took nothing for

99

granted, left nothing for chance. Every line of his score was planned and motivated. And he kept on working on the most minute details of his work not only up to the very moment he dispatched the manuscript to me, but even afterwards. After I had given the première of the work I received a frantic wire from him: "In my delight, completely forgot to suggest you raise bass of bar 341 to D-sharp, which then slides into E-natural of bar 345 unnoticeably." He followed his wire with a voluminous letter in which he pointed out to me, bar by bar, sometimes note by note, what sounded well, and what didn't, and what we should do about it.

Mark Twain: A Portrait for Orchestra was introduced by the Cincinnati Symphony Orchestra in Cincinnati on May 14, 1942. Kostelanetz conducted. It was repeated over the Columbia Broadcasting network, once again under Kostelanetz, on June 7. Reviewing the latter performance, Robert Lawrence wrote in the New York *Herald Tribune* that the work "offered much that made for good basic listening. This seemed not to be music aimed at intellect. It avoided contrapuntal forms, placing its reliance on melodic, harmonic, and emotional appeal. . . . It is pleasant, once in a while, not to be fugally overwhelmed, and Mr. Kern's approach for its own purposes must be accounted a success."

This "portrait" is in four sections (or episodes). The first, "Hannibal Days," tells of Twain's youthful days on the Mississippi when the steamboat would arrive to arouse the sleepy town and inject a brief interlude of

excitement. In "Gorgeous Pilot House," Twain leaves his home and boyhood behind him and becomes a pilot's assistant. It is the time of the Civil War. In the third episode, "Wandering Westward," Twain becomes a prospector in Nevada. It is his failure as a miner that leads him to enter upon journalism in the West. The concluding part of the portrait is "Mark in Eruption." Twain is now an established writer, the recipient of many honors in this country and Europe. The portrait ends with a recollection of the music heard in the first part, descriptive of the Mississippi River: though world-famous, Twain has not forgotten the river at whose banks he spent the carefree days of boyhood.

Both *Scenario* and *Mark Twain* are works that are simple, pleasant to listen to, and filled with harmonic sweetness and melodic charm. But neither work is a great piece of music or an important one; and no one knew this better than Kern himself. He was essentially a miniaturist. He was not at ease in the larger forms in the way he was when writing a song. He had had no experience in developing musical ideas into spacious contours and he was awkward trying to do so. He did not write as naturally for the instruments of the orchestra as he did for the voice. Though he had had some help in instrumentation, it frequently sounds labored. In the last analysis, both of his large works are the sum of ingratiating melodic parts; but it must be said that at all times the parts are better than the whole.

101

CHAPTER SIXTEEN

Paris: 1942

BUT the finest piece of music written by Kern during this period was not one of his ambitious symphonic works but (as you might expect) a song.

In several ways, this song was a phenomenon among Kern's compositions. It was the only important Kern song in which the lyric came before the melody, the lyric dictating the sentiment and structure of the tune. It was the only important song ever written by Kern that was not originally intended for a specific play or motion picture. It was also one of a scattered few of his songs inspired by a historic event, born out of the storms and stresses of the era in which it was conceived, the poignant aftermath of one of the most tragic events of our times.

The song, of course, was "The Last Time I Saw

Paris," inspired by the invasion of Paris by the Nazis during the early years of World War II.

This is the way the song came to be written.

Oscar Hammerstein's depression over the fall of Paris made it impossible for him to work. Anybody who knew Paris the way Hammerstein did, and loved it as he did, could not fail to be stirred to the very depths of his being. It has been said that Paris is the only city in the world that a man can love the way he does a woman. Every part of Paris was dear to Hammerstein—from the funny, irregular chimneys on the housetops to the broad boulevards; from the noble Notre Dame Cathedral to the humblest street café; from the magnificence of Maxim's on Rue Royale to the sordidness of an apache-haunt on Rue du Lappe; from the magnificent Opéra, rich with century-old traditions, down to the bawdy songs of the café-chantant, the popular tunes of the street singer accompanied by an accordion, and the peculiar squeaks from the horns of decrepit taxicabs.

Paris was all this and much more. It was the place where democracy was born in the throes of the Revolution, and where, ever since, tolerance and freedom would always find a home. It was the source of so many progressive movements in literature, music, and painting, the breeding ground for artistic and aesthetic cults and vogues from Impressionism to Existentialism, a veritable haven of the spirit.

That the Nazis were now in Paris, trampling with bloodstained boots on all those things which for so many years had been the pride and hope and love of civilized men the world over, was a crushing blow. It was such a blow to Hammerstein. There was only one way he could sublimate his aroused feelings, and that was by writing a song lyric about that tragic event.

He went to California and gave Kern the lyric he had written in New York.

It was a tender elegy whose strength lay in its simplicity, and its beauty in its heartfelt sincerity. It touched Kern, and he said so. He had never before written a song without the stimulus of dramatic action, but he had complete faith that he could do it.

"I'd like to try right now, Oscar. Read me that lyric again," he said.

As Hammerstein slowly reread his verse, Kern started working out a melodic idea on the piano. The melody came quickly—melodies always did with Kern—and by the time he had finished molding and shaping it, the tune matched the lyric in simplicity and emotional genuineness.

"I think I have it now, Oscar," Kern said at last. "If you'll hold on a moment I'll play it for you."

When Kern finished playing the song, Hammerstein told him, "Thanks, Jerry. You've done me a great personal favor. But you've also done yourself a favor, too. You've just written one of your finest songs, and it will be immortal."

It was not only one of Kern's best songs but also one of his most successful. It was one of the few great songs to emerge from World War II, and by which that war will be remembered by future generations. It caught and translated the emotions of the times. Whenever it was sung—and it was sung with tremendous success by such night-club entertainers as Hildegarde and Sophie Tucker—it invariably inspired tears and cheers. (The American writer, Elliot Paul, borrowed the title of the song—and quoted the lyric in his frontispiece—for his finest book, a panorama of life on a single Paris street called *The Last Time I Saw Paris*).

Though "The Last Time I Saw Paris" was written by Hammerstein and Kern independently of any stage or screen production, it was soon incorporated into a screen musical, *Lady Be Good*, a Gershwin musical comedy adapted for the screen. It was the only song by Kern in the entire production, but it won that year the award of the Motion Picture Academy.

CHAPTER SEVENTEEN

Good-by, Mr. Kern

KERN wrote his last score for the motion pictures in 1945. It was *Centennial Summer*, a 20th Century-Fox production starring Jeanne Crain, Linda Darnell, and Cornel Wilde. In some respects it was one of the best he had written for the screen, including as it did two Kern gems, "All Through the Day" and "In Love in Vain."

The year of 1945 was a big one for Kern. His sixtieth birthday was the cause of nation-wide celebration. For forty-one years he had been writing more and better songs (over one thousand!) and more and better scores for the theater and motion pictures (over one hundred) than any other American. For over twenty years he had seen service on the Board of Directors of ASCAP—the American Society of Composers, Authors and Publishers. In 1944 he had been elected to the National Institute of Arts and Letters. He was also vice-president and part owner of the great publishing house of Harms. He was, deservedly, a national figure in American music. Accordingly his birthday was celebrated everywhere with commemorative broadcasts, performances, and magazine articles.

These tributes and honors looked to Kern's past. But Kern himself was looking into the future. He was as always involved in many new projects and assignments. On Broadway the groundwork had been laid for a new revival of *Show Boat*. At the same time discussions had begun for a new Kern musical, the first in six years, to be produced on the Broadway stage by Oscar Hammerstein, 2d, and Richard Rodgers, and based on the story of Annie Oakley. In Hollywood plans were drawn up to film the story of his life (the story to be written by one of his old collaborators, Guy Bolton). Only this film biography did Kern regard skeptically and without enthusiasm. His modesty refused to permit him to believe that his story could be of interest on the screen. "I'm too normal," was the way he put it, "and I lead too dull and uneventful a life to make a good picture. I've had only one wife and the studio feels that I need more women in the past, so they've stuck in as many as they liked." To Guy Bolton he said, "If your story tells the truth it will be the dullest picture in the world."

The Broadway projects excited him much more. *Show Boat*, after all, was his first love, and he was thrilled to return to the living theater. But he was even more aroused by the plan to write a new musical for Broadway. He had been working for the screen too long, and he was nostalgic for the excitement and exhilaration that attended the preparation of a live show for Broadway.

He came back to Broadway late in 1945 to help supervise the *Show Boat* production and to conclude negotiations for his new musical. At sixty, he felt that he was at the height of his productive powers, that there was much more he still had to contribute both to music and to the theater.

But he did not live to make that contribution.

On the morning of November 5, he collapsed in front of 450 Park Avenue. He had not been sick. Deems Taylor, who had seen him a few weeks earlier, had remarked at the time that he had never before seen "a more alert, vigorous, and happy man." The stroke (for that is what it was) came without warning. Half an hour earlier he had been in a cheerful mood, looking forward zestfully to the auditioning of new singers for the *Show Boat* revival.

Suddenly he had become seriously ill. For a few days he was in an oxygen tent in the Doctors Hospital, first rallying slightly, then taking alarming turns for the worse. But he never regained consciousness. Oscar Hammerstein, 2d, took a room in the hospital to be near him night and day.

The end came on Sunday afternoon, November 11, at 1:10 P.M. His wife, daughter, and Oscar Hammerstein were with him in his last hours. Irving Berlin, who came to the hospital at this time to visit Kern, was told the sad news that Kern was no longer alive. (It was Berlin who was to write the music for the show planned for Kern's return to Broadway and who realized with that show one of his greatest hits, *Annie Get Your Gun.*)

No sooner did the bulletin bring the news over the radio networks when the mourning became nation-wide. There were many who had been close friends. To them the loss was personal and irreparable. Numerous others had known him only casually, and they, too, felt the loss keenly. To the countless millions who had never met him or even seen him—but had known him all the years only through his wonderful songs—it was as if a part of America had died with him.

Deems Taylor put it this way:

> We have not even the consolation of knowing that his work was done. . . . Kern was sixty, which means he had easily a score of years of his music still to write. Now we shall never hear it.

The night of Kern's death, radio stations throughout the country held commemorative programs to honor his memory. For the rest of the week Kern's music was heard again and again, and through every possible medium, as if to remind his grieving admirers everywhere of all the things he was.

From Washington, D. C., came the following message from President Truman:

His melodies, surviving him, will live in our voices and warm our hearts for many years to come, for they are the kind of simple, honest songs that belong to no time or fashion. The man who gave them to us earned a lasting place in his nation's memory.

The funeral services at the Ferncliff Cemetery in Ardsley, New York, were simple. His family wanted it that way because they knew that if he could have expressed a wish he would have preferred a modest and unostentatious send-off. But all his close friends from Broadway and Hollywood were there to mourn his passing, and they included all the great and near-great of the entertainment world.

His friend and attorney, Mark Holstein, read the 23rd and 90th Psalms. And his friend and collaborator, Oscar Hammerstein, 2d, delivered the touching eulogy:

We all know in our hearts that these few minutes we devote to him now are small drops in the ocean of our affections. Our real tribute will be paid over many years of remembering, of telling good stories about him, and thinking about him when we are by ourselves.

We, in this chapel, will cherish our special knowledge of this world figure. We will remember a jaunty, happy man whose sixty years were crowded with success and fun and love. Let us thank whatever God we believe in that we shared some part of the good, bright life Jerry led on this earth.

111

CHAPTER EIGHTEEN

"He Jes' Keeps Rollin' Along"

JEROME KERN was dead—but his music, never! If there was any further proof needed of the immense vitality of his songs it was forthcoming in the years following his death. There could no longer be any new Kern songs; but the old ones returned in Hollywood, over the air waves, on phonograph records, in theaters (in short, wherever a popular song is heard), as fresh and as lovable as the day they were written.

On December 9, 1945, there took place a special Jerome Kern program sponsored by ASCAP over the CBS network. The foremost personalities of stage, screen, night club, and radio collaborated. Hildegarde sang the song she helped make famous, "The Last Time I Saw Paris." Judy Garland did "Look for the Silver Lining," and Frank Sinatra performed songs from *Show Boat* and *Music in the Air*. Others who participated in-

113

cluded Bing Crosby, Nelson Eddy, Patrice Munsel, Dinah Shore, and many others. The National Broadcasting Company also put on a mammoth show to honor the composer.

In 1946 Frank Black introduced over the NBC network a serious piece of music by Robert Russell Bennett called *Symphonic Story*. It was an elaborate symphonic treatment of Kern's most famous tunes. In the same year Kern's screen musical, *Can't Help Singing,* was released nationally and *Show Boat* was successfully revived on Broadway.

In 1948 the screen biography of Kern, *Till the Clouds Roll By,* was seen in the motion-picture theaters throughout the country. Any similarity between this film biography and Kern's life was purely coincidental. But the parade of wonderful songs, the picked fruit of a fertile career, made this one of the best musicals of the year: it contained his first song to be heard on Broadway, "How'd You Like to Spoon with Me," his most famous songs from *Show Boat, Sunny, Sally, Roberta, Cover Girl, Swing Time,* and "The Last Time I Saw Paris." Still another musical film was seen that year in which three popular Kern tunes were featured prominently. The film, *Look for the Silver Lining,* was the biography of Marilyn Miller, and the songs were "Who?" "Sunny," and "Look for the Silver Lining." There was still another poignant reminder of Marilyn Miller—and of Kern—and in the Broadway revival of

Sally with Bambi Lynn in the Marilyn Miller role and Willie Howard. Critics found Kern's music as fresh and as captivating as ever.

In 1951 *Music in the Air* was brought back to Broadway with a cast including Dennis King, Jane Pickens, Charles Winninger, and Conrad Nagel. The show was described by Wolcott Gibbs of *The New Yorker* as "engaging," due primarily to the score which "is among the most charming ever written." Brooks Atkinson wrote in the New York *Times:* "Although ours is a graceless world, the lovely Kern score is still full of friendship, patience, cheerfulness, and pleasure."

Early in 1952, two Kern musicals were seen in new screen versions: *Show Boat* and *Roberta* (the latter retitled *Lovely to Look At,* now starring Kathryn Grayson and Red Skelton).

On July 12, 1952, an all-Jerome Kern concert was heard for the first time at the Lewisohn Stadium concerts in New York City. The program included a condensed concert version of *Show Boat,* together with hit songs from five other Kern musicals, and the *Mark Twain* portrait. This concert was heard by the largest audience to attend a Lewisohn Stadium concert that season—19,000. The enthusiasm generated by Kern's music gave hope and promise that this concert would henceforth be a regular event at the Stadium (and probably elsewhere too), a fitting rival to the now traditional Gershwin Nights.

Jerome Kern dead? Not so long as his music remains such a vital, throbbing part of the American scene. Only Kern's ashes were buried at the Ferncliff crematory on that sad afternoon in 1945. His spirit has remained with us ever since and has become an inextricable part of American culture, of the American heritage.

Appendixes

1. A Select List of Broadway Productions for Which Jerome Kern Wrote the Complete Score

2. A Select List of Broadway Productions in Which Jerome Kern Songs Were Interpolated

3. Motion Pictures for Which Jerome Kern Wrote the Complete Score

4. Motion Pictures in Which Jerome Kern Songs Were Interpolated

5. The Fifty Greatest Songs of Jerome Kern

6. Recommended Recordings of Music by Jerome Kern

Appendix 1

A Select List of Broadway Productions for Which
Jerome Kern Wrote the Complete Score

1911 LA BELLE PAREE

1912 THE RED PETTICOAT

1913 OH I SAY

1914 THE GIRL FROM UTAH

1915 90 IN THE SHADE
      NOBODY HOME
      VERY GOOD, EDDIE

1917 HAVE A HEART
      LOVE O' MIKE
      OH BOY!
      LEAVE IT TO JANE
      MISS 1917

119

1918 OH LADY! LADY!
OH MY DEAR
TOOT-TOOT
ROCK-A-BYE BABY
HEAD OVER HEELS

1919 SHE'S A GOOD FELLOW
ZIP GOES A MILLION

1920 THE NIGHT BOAT
HITCHY-KOO OF 1920
SALLY

1921 GOOD MORNING DEARIE

1922 THE BUNCH AND JUDY

1923 STEPPING STONES

1924 SITTING PRETTY
DEAR SIR

1925 SUNNY
THE CITY CHAP

1926 CRISS CROSS

1927 SHOW BOAT

Appendix 1

1929 SWEET ADELINE

1931 THE CAT AND THE FIDDLE

1932 MUSIC IN THE AIR

1933 ROBERTA

1939 VERY WARM FOR MAY

Appendix 2

A Select List of Broadway Productions in Which
Jerome Kern Songs Were Interpolated

1905   THE EARL AND THE GIRL

1906   THE RICH MR. HOGGENHEIMER

1907   PETER PAN
        THE DAIRY MAIDS
        FASCINATING FLORA
        FLUFFY RUFFLES

1908   THE GIRLS OF GOTENBURG
        THE ORCHID
        THE WALTZ DREAM

1909   THE DOLLAR PRINCESS
        THE GIRL AND THE WIZARD

1910   MR. WIX OF WICKHAM
        THE KING OF CADONIA

1911 LITTLE MISS FIX-IT
THE HEN-PECKS
THE KISS WALTZ
THE SIREN

1912 THE GIRL FROM MONTMARTRE
MIND THE PAINT GIRL
THE POLISH WEDDING

1913 THE DOLL GIRL
THE MARRIAGE MARKET

1914 THE LAUGHING HUSBAND

1915 COUSIN LUCY

1916 MISS SPRINGTIME
ZIEGFELD FOLLIES OF 1916

1917 THE RIVIERA GIRL
ZIEGFELD FOLLIES OF 1917

1918 THE CANARY

1919 LOOK WHO'S HERE

1920 THE CHARM SCHOOL

1921 ZIEGFELD FOLLIES OF 1921

1923   THE ROSE BRIAR

1929   MAMBA'S DAUGHTERS

1930   RIPPLES

Appendix 3

~~~~~~

*Motion Pictures for Which Jerome Kern Wrote the
Complete Score*

1929   SHOW BOAT *(Universal)*
        SALLY *(First National)*

1930   SUNNY *(First National)*

1931   MEN OF THE SKY *(MGM)*

1933   THE CAT AND THE FIDDLE *(MGM)*

1934   MUSIC IN THE AIR *(RKO)*
        ROBERTA *(RKO)*
        SWEET ADELINE *(Warners)*

1936   SWING TIME *(RKO)*
        SHOW BOAT *(Universal)*

1937   HIGH, WIDE, AND HANDSOME *(Paramount)*

1938 JOY OF LIVING *(RKO)*

1941 SUNNY *(RKO)*

1942 YOU WERE NEVER LOVELIER *(Columbia)*

1944 CAN'T HELP SINGING *(Universal)*
      COVER GIRL *(Columbia)*

1946 CENTENNIAL SUMMER *(20th Century-Fox)*
      TILL THE CLOUDS ROLL BY *(Warners)*

1952 SHOW BOAT *(MGM)*
      LOVELY TO LOOK AT *(MGM)*

Appendix 4

Motion Pictures in Which Jerome Kern Songs
Were Interpolated

1930 THREE SISTERS *(Fox)*
"Lonely Feet"

1935 RECKLESS *(MGM)*
"Reckless"

1937 WHEN YOU'RE IN LOVE *(Columbia)*
"Our Song"
"Whistling Boy"

1940 ONE NIGHT IN THE TROPICS *(Universal)*
"Back in My Shell"
"Remind Me"
"You and Your Kiss"

1941 LADY BE GOOD *(MGM)*
"The Last Time I Saw Paris"

1944 SONG OF RUSSIA *(MGM)*
      "And Russia Is Her Name"

1949 LOOK FOR THE SILVER LINING *(Warners)*
      "Who"
      "Sunny"
      "Look for the Silver Lining"

Appendix 5

The Fifty Greatest Songs of Jerome Kern

1914 THE GIRL FROM UTAH
"They Didn't Believe Me"
"You're Here and I'm Here"
"I'd Like to Wander"

1915 VERY GOOD, EDDIE
"Babes in the Woods"
"I've Got to Dance"

1917 OH BOY!
"Magic Melody"
"Till the Clouds Roll By"

LEAVE IT TO JANE
"Leave It to Jane"
"Siren's Song"
"The Sun Shines Brighter"

1920 SALLY
"Look for the Silver Lining"
"A Wild, Wild Rose"

1921 GOOD MORNING DEARIE
"Kalua"

1925 SUNNY
"Who"
"Sunny"

1927 SHOW BOAT
"Make Believe"
"Ol' Man River"
"Can't Help Lovin' Dat Man"
"You Are Love"
"Why Do I Love You"
"Bill"

1929 SWEET ADELINE
"Here Am I"
"Why Was I Born?"
"Don't Ever Leave Me"

1931 THE CAT AND THE FIDDLE
"She Didn't Say Yes"
"The Night Was Made for Love"

1932 MUSIC IN THE AIR
"I've Told Ev'ry Little Star"
"The Song Is You"

1933 ROBERTA
      "Yesterdays"
      "Smoke Gets in Your Eyes"
      "The Touch of Your Hand"
      "Lovely to Look At"

1934 ROBERTA (screen version)
      "One More Dance" (Also titled "Night Flies By")
      "I Won't Dance"

1935 I DREAM TOO MUCH
      "I Dream Too Much"
      "Jockey on the Carousel"

1936 SWING TIME
      "The Way You Look Tonight"
      "A Fine Romance"

1937 WHEN YOU'RE IN LOVE
      "Our Song"
      HIGH, WIDE AND HANDSOME
      "Can I Forget You?"

1939 VERY WARM FOR MAY
      "All the Things You Are"

1941 LADY BE GOOD
      "The Last Time I Saw Paris"

1942 YOU WERE NEVER LOVELIER
      "Dearly Beloved"
      "You Were Never Lovelier"
      "On the Beam"

1944 CAN'T HELP SINGING
      "More and More"

      COVER GIRL
      "Any Moment Now"
      "Long Ago and Far Away"

1946 CENTENNIAL SUMMER
      "In Love in Vain"
      "All Through the Day"

Appendix 6

Recommended Recordings of Music by Jerome Kern

I. SYMPHONIC WORKS

Mark Twain: A Portrait for Orchestra. André Kostelanetz and his orchestra. Columbia cl-864.

Scenario for Orchestra. Philadelphia Pops Orchestra conducted by André Kostelanetz. Columbia l-806.

II. MUSICAL COMEDY AND MOTION PICTURE SCORES

Music in the Air. Al Goodman's Orchestra with the Guild Choristers, Jane Pickens, and other vocalists. Victor lk-1025.

CONTENTS: Overture; I've Told Ev'ry Little Star; Prayer; There's a Hill Beyond a Hill; I'm Alone; I'm So Eager; One More Dance; In Egern on the Tegern See; The Song Is You; We Belong Together

Roberta. Al Goodman's Orchestra with the Guild Choristers, Marion Bell, Eve Young, Jimmy Carroll, Ray Charles. Victor LK-1007.

CONTENTS: Let's Begin; You're Devastating; Yesterdays; I Won't Dance; The Touch of Your Hand; Lovely to Look At; Smoke Gets In Your Eyes; Something Had to Happen.

Roberta (motion picture title, *Lovely to Look At*). Joan Roberts, Jack Cassidy, Kaye Ballard, and other vocalists with chorus and orchestra conducted by Lehman Engel. Columbia CL-6220.

CONTENTS: Smoke Gets In Your Eyes; Yesterdays; The Touch of Your Hand; You're Devastating; I Won't Dance; Let's Begin; I'll Be Hard to Handle; Lovely to Look At.

Show Boat. Robert Merrill, Patrice Munsel, Risë Stevens, Janet Pavek, Kevin Scott, Katherine Graves, and chorus and orchestra conducted by Lehman Engel. Victor LM-2008. This recording is virtually the entire score, with only minor deletions.

Show Boat. Jan Clayton, Charles Fredericks, Carol Bruce, Kenneth Spencer. Columbia OL-4058.

> CONTENTS: Overture; Cotton Blossom; Make Believe; Ol' Man River; Can't Help Lovin' Dat Man; Life Upon the Wicked Stage; You Are Love; Why Do I Love You?; Bill; Nobody Else But Me.

Show Boat. Sound track of the MGM motion picture released in 1951, starring Kathryn Grayson, William Warfield, and Howard Keel. MGM-3230.

> CONTENTS: Why Do I Love You?; Make Believe; Ol' Man River; Can't Help Lovin' Dat Man; Bill.

Show Boat. SEE *Scenario for Orchestra* (Symphonic Works).

Till the Clouds Roll By. Sound track of the MGM production of Jerome Kern's life, starring Robert Walker, Judy Garland, Dinah Shore, June Allyson, Frank Sinatra, and many others. MGM-501.

> CONTENTS: Make Believe; Can't Help Lovin' Dat Man; Ol' Man River; Till the Clouds Roll By; How'd You Like to Spoon With Me?; They Didn't Believe Me; The Last Time I Saw Paris; I Won't Dance; Why Was I Born?; Smoke Gets In Your Eyes; Who?; Look For the Silver Lining; Sunny; Cleopatterer; Leave It to Jane; Go Little Boat; One More Dance; Land Where the Good Songs Go; Yesterdays; Long Ago and

Far Away; A Fine Romance; All the Things You Are; She Didn't Say Yes.

III. SONG COLLECTIONS

Kostelanetz Conducts Broadway and Movie Favorites. André Kostelanetz and his orchestra. Columbia CB-11.

CONTENTS: This album includes the following songs by Kern: I've Told Ev'ry Little Star; The Song Is You; Why Was I Born?; The Way You Look Tonight.

Music of Jerome Kern. Stanley Black and the Kingsway Promenade Orchestra. London LL-579.

CONTENTS: Don't Ever Leave Me; They Didn't Believe Me; Who?; I've Told Ev'ry Little Star; The Touch of Your Hand; High, Wide and Handsome; Kalua; In Egern on Tegern See; The Way You Look Tonight; The Song Is You; Smoke Gets In Your Eyes; I Won't Dance; Look for the Silver Lining.

Music of Jerome Kern. Bing Crosby, Dixie Lee Crosby, and orchestra. Decca A-5001.

CONTENTS: Till the Clouds Roll By; Ol' Man River; I've Told Ev'ry Little Star; Dearly Beloved; All Through the Night; A Fine Romance; The Way You Look Tonight.

138

Appendix 6

Music of Jerome Kern. André Kostelanetz and his orchestra. CL-776.

> CONTENTS: Smoke Gets In Your Eyes; I've Told Ev'ry Little Star; The Song Is You; Yesterdays; You Are Love; Make Believe; Ol' Man River; She Didn't Say Yes; All the Things You Are; They Didn't Believe Me; The Night Was Made for Love; Look for the Silver Lining; The Jockey on the Carousel; The Way You Look Tonight; I Dream Too Much; Long Ago and Far Away; Why Was I Born?; Why Do I Love You?.

Music of Jerome Kern. Gordon String Quartet. Decca A-5143.

> CONTENTS: All the Things You Are; The Way You Look Tonight; Smoke Gets In Your Eyes; Yesterdays; Once in a Blue Moon; The Song Is You; Bill.

A Memo From Jerome Kern. Sung by George Byron, with piano accompaniment. Desto D-501.

> CONTENTS: Moon Song; Remind Me; Sweetest Sight; More and More; Poor Pierrot; Can I Forget You?; Up with the Lark.

The Columbia Album of Jerome Kern. Paul Weston and his orchestra. Columbia C2L-2.

> CONTENTS: Smoke Gets In Your Eyes; You are Love; She Didn't Say Yes; They Didn't Believe Me; Why

139

Was I Born?; Who?; Yesterdays; All the Things You Are; Why Do I Love You?; The Touch of Your Hand; Look for the Silver Lining; The Song Is You; Can I Forget You?; Just Let Me Look at You; Lovely to Look At; In Love in Vain; I Dream Too Much; Long Ago and Far Away; The Folks Who Live on the Hill; All Through the Day; The Way You Look Tonight; Dearly Beloved; I'm Old Fashioned; A Fine Romance.

Index

Academy of Music: 31
Adams, Franklin P.: 94
Adams, Maud: 40
Ade, George: 57
Alvin Theatre: 81, 83
Annie Get Your Gun: 109-110
Arden, Eve: 83
ASCAP: 107, 112
Astaire, Fred: 86
Atkinson, Brooks: 81, 83, 115

Bach: 4
Ball, Ernest R.: 35
Bartholomae, Philip: 45
Bayes, Nora: 42
Beethoven: 4, 14
Benchley, Robert: 82
Bennett, Robert Russell: 96, 114
Berlin, Irving: 6, 8, 25, 94, 109-110
Bernard, Sam: 39
Black, Frank: 114
Bland, James A.: 6
Bledsoe, Jules: 71
Boles, John: 86
Bolm, Adolf: 57

Bolton, Guy: 44-47, 56-58, 108
Brahms: 4
Brian, Donald: 42, 83
Brice, Fanny: 56
Broder and Schlam: 30
Bruce, Carol: 77
Burns, Robert: 53
Butterworth, Charles: 79, 86

Carlisle, Margaret: 76
Carminati, Tullio: 81
Carnegie Hall: 3, 95-97
Carrington, Katherine: 81
Casino Theatre: 77
Castle, Irene: 57
Chapman, John: 78
Chopin: 14
Churchill, Winston: 97
Cincinnati Symphony Orchestra: 100
Claire, Ina: 56
Clayton, Jan: 77
Cleveland Orchestra: 96-97
Cohan, George M.: 34, 42
Coleridge: 52
Comstock, F. Ray: 45

Index

Copland, Aaron: 99
Crain, Jeanne: 86, 107
Crosby, Bing: 114

Dale, Alan: 40, 73
Darnell, Linda: 86, 107
Davies, Marion: 56
Debussy: 4
DeSylva, Buddy: 58
Downes, Olin: 76, 98
Dreiser, Theodore: 34
Dresser, Paul: 34, 37
Dressler, Marie: 39
Dreyfus, Max: 37-39, 54
Duff Gordon, Lady: 57
Dunne, Irene: 76, 77, 86-87
Durbin, Deanna: 86

Eddy, Nelson: 114
Edwards, Gus: 33

Fairbanks, Douglas, Jr.: 86
Fall, Leo: 40
Feist, Leo: 31
Ferber, Edna: 63-66, 68
Fields, Lew: 42, 57
Fields, W. C.: 56
Fisher, Fred: 59
Fisher, Irving: 58
Foster, Stephen: 6
Foy, Eddie: 26
Frawley, Paul: 59
Fredericks, Charles: 77
Friml, Rudolf: 38, 60, 62
Frohman, Charles K.: 24-26, 46, 49, 51

Gadski, Mme. Johanna: 4-5
Gallico, Paolo: 19
Gallico, Paul: 19
Gardella, Tess: 77
Gardner, Ava: 77
Garland, Judy: 113
Garland, Robert: 73
Gershwin, George: 8, 25, 38, 57, 106, 115

Gibbs, Wolcott: 115
Globe Theatre: 80
Goldsmith, Oliver: 52
Gordon String Quartet: 96
Gounod: 4
Grayson, Kathryn: 77, 115
Grey, Clifford: 58
Green, Schuyler: 45

Hall, Bettina: 80
Hall, Natalie: 81
Hammerstein, Arthur: 60, 79
Hammerstein, Oscar, 2d: 60-62, 66-70, 72, 75-76, 78-81, 86, 91, 104-106, 109-111
Hammerstein Theatre: 79
Harbach, Otto: 60-62, 80, 82
Hardy, Thomas: 52
Harkrider, John: 71
Harms Publishing Company: 37-39, 43, 108
Harris, Charles K.: 30, 31
Haydn: 4
Hayworth, Rita: 86
Heidelberg: 23
Herbert, Victor: 6-7, 34, 43
Hersholt, Jean: 86
Hildegarde: 106, 113
Holstein, Mark: 111
Hope, Bob: 83
Hopper, Edna Wallace: 39
Howard, Willie: 115
Howley and Haviland: 37-38
Hurtig and Seamon Theatre: 33

Johnson, Samuel: 52
Jolson, Al: 41
Jones, Allan: 77, 82, 86
Jones, Sydney: 42
Joyce, Peggy Hopkins: 57

Keats: 52
Keel, Howard: 77
Kelly, Nancy: 86

Index

Kern, Elizabeth Jane (daughter): 89

Kern, Eva Leale (wife): 50

Kern, Fanny (mother): 13-17, 20, 27-29

Kern, Henry (father): 13-22

Kern, Jerome: accidental discovery of vocation, 24-28; ambition to be good composer, 28, 36-37, 64-65; birth, 15; as book-collector, 52-53; career in Hollywood, 85-89, 107, 109; career in Tin Pan Alley, 5, 7, 29-40; collaboration with Bolton, 44, 56-57, 108; collaboration with Hammerstein, 60-62, 66-68, 75-76, 79-81, 91-92, 105; collaboration with Wodehouse, 44, 56-57; conservatory training, 8, 23; as craftsman, 9; death and burial, 109-111, 116; discovery by Max Dreyfus, 38-39, 54; early success on Broadway, 40-47; emergence from Tin Pan Alley, 7-8; evaluation of his genius, 3-5, 11; facility as composer, 55, 67; family life as child, 13-15; fifty greatest songs, list, 131-134; first business experience, 20-22, 49; first published song, 26; growing up in Newark, 15-22; his favorite song, 82, 94; his influence on musical theater, 6, 9-11, 44-46, 63-64, 75-76; honors, 107-108, 110-111; Jerome Kern Jubilee Week, 95; last Broadway production, 79-83; life in Beverly Hills, 89-94; life in Bronxville, 47; list of Broadway productions, 119-125; list of motion pictures, 127-130; luck, 49-54; musical aspirations, 17-19; nation-wide hits, 43; at New York College of Music, 19-20; "a node in the vibrations of the 19th century," 15; originality of his music, 40; personality, 16, 36, 49, 87-88, 92-94; piano piece, 37; pioneer in musical comedy, 10-11; Princess Theatre Shows, 11, 44-46, 57, 63; recommended recordings, 135-141; Rodgers' debt to, 9-10; salesman for Harms, 39; screen biography, 108, 114; sense of humor, 94; shortcomings as serious composer, 23-24; Show Boat, 4, 62-78, 96-97; sixtieth birthday, 107-108; in stock market, 53; study in Europe, 19, 22-27; success, 5-6, 41-47, 55-59, 73-78; symphonic works, 3, 23, 77-78, 96-101, 114, 135; talent, 55-56; total achievement, 107-108; true artist, 8-9, 75-76; Victor Herbert's successor, 43; way of working, 90-93, 99-100; work for Frohman, 24-26, 46, 49

Kern Broadway productions: complete list, 119-125; The Cat and the Fiddle, 11, 80; The Girl from Utah, 42-43; Good Morning, Dearie, 58-59; Have a Heart, 46; La Belle Paree, 41-42; Leave It to Jane, 57; Love o' Mike, 10; Miss 1917, 56-57; Mr. Wix of Wickersham, 40; Music in the Air, 11, 80-81, 95, 113, 115; 90 in the Shade, 44; Nobody Home, 44-46; Oh Boy, 57; Oh I Say, 42; The Red Petticoat, 42; Roberta, 82, 114-115; Sally, 58, 114, 115; Show Boat, 4, 11, 62-78, 95, 97, 108-109, 113-115; Sitting Pretty, 59; Stepping Stones, 59; Sunny, 59-60, 114; Sweet Adeline, 79; Very Good, Eddie, 10, 45-46; Very Warm for May, 83; Ziegfeld Follies, 56

Index

Kern motion pictures: 85-89, 107; complete list, 127-130; *Can't Help Singing*, 86, 114; *Centennial Summer*, 86, 107; *Cover Girl*, 86, 114; *I Dream Too Much*, 86-88; *Look for the Silver Lining*, 114; *Lovely to Look At*, 115; *Music in the Air*, 86; *Roberta*, 86, 115; *Sally*, 85; *Show Boat*, 77, 85, 87, 115; *Sunny*, 85, 87; *Sweet Adeline*, 87; *Swing Time*, 86, 96, 114; *When You're in Love*, 86; *You Were Never Lovelier*, 86

Kern orchestral works: 3, 23, 77-78, 96-101, 135; *Mark Twain*, 98-101, 115; *Scenario*, 96-98

Kern recordings, list of: 135-141

Kern songs: List of fifty greatest, 131-134; "All the Things You Are," 8, 83; "Bill," 8, 68, 73; "Can't Help Lovin' Dat Man," 72-73, 97; "How'd You Like to Spoon with Me?," 26, 37, 114; "I Dream Too Much," 88; "I've Told Ev'ry Little Star," 81; "Kalua," 59; "The Last Time I Saw Paris," 103-106, 113, 114; "Look for the Silver Lining," 8, 58, 113, 114; "Magic Melody," 8, 57; "Make Believe," 72, 97; "The Night Was Made for Love," 80; "Ol' Man River," 67-68, 97; "She Didn't Say Yes," 80; "Smoke Gets in Your Eyes," 4, 8, 82, 94; "The Song Is You," 81, 96; "Sunny," 114; "They Didn't Believe Me," 8, 43; "Till the Clouds Roll By," 57; "The Touch of Your Hand," 82; "The Way You Look Tonight," 86, 92, 96; "Who," 59, 114; "Why Do I Love You?,"

73, 97; "Yesterdays," 82; "You Are Love," 73; "You're Here and I'm Here," 8

King, Dennis: 77, 115
Kostelanetz, André: 87-88, 98-100
Kummer, Clare: 44

Lady Be Good: 106
Lambert, Alexander: 19
La Plante, Laura: 77
Lardner, Ring: 45
Laska, Edward: 26
Lawrence, Robert: 100
Lewisohn Stadium: 77-78, 115
Liszt: 14
London: 24-27, 49-51, 59, 73
Long, Avon: 83
Lusitania: 51
Lyceum Publishing Company: 29
Lynn, Bambi: 115
Lyric Theatre: 60

MacDonald, Jeanette: 86
Main, Marjorie: 81
Manhattan Opera Company: 60
Marks, E. B.: 37
Marsh, Howard: 71
Maxine Elliott Theatre: 10
Meader, George: 80
Metaxa, Georges: 80
Metropolitan Opera: 60
Milhaud: 4
Miller, Alice Duer: 82
Miller, Marilyn: 58-59, 85, 114-115
Moore, Grace: 59, 86
Morgan, Frank: 86
Morgan, Helen: 71, 77, 79
Motion Picture Academy Award: 86, 92, 106
Motion pictures: 77, 85-89, 96, 107, 114-115, 127-130
Mozart: 4, 16

Index

Munsel, Patrice: 114
Music, popular: may be good, 3-5; methods of promotion, 32-34; Tin Pan Alley formula, 32-33; use of song-pluggers, 32-34; use of song slides to plug, 33
Musical comedy: Kern's share in shaping, 6, 9-11, 44-46, 63-64, 80; large investment necessary, 64; *Show Boat* as new development, 71, 73-76. *Also see* Kern Broadway productions
Myrtil, Odette: 80

Nagel, Conrad: 115
National Institute of Arts and Letters: 107-108
Navarro, Ramon: 86
New York *American*: 73
New York College of Music: 19-20
New York *Herald Tribune*: 73, 98, 100
New York Philharmonic-Symphony Orchestra: 97
New York *Telegram*: 73
New York *Times*: 9-10, 76, 81-82, 98, 115
New York *World*: 73
New Yorker, The: 81, 115
Norworth, Jack: 42

Oakley, Annie: 108
Offenbach: 4
Oklahoma!: 9
Oliver, Edna May: 71

Palace Theatre: 4
Paris: 103-106
Paul, Elliot: 106
Pennington, Ann: 57
Philadelphia Orchestra: 96
Pickens, Jane: 115
Pierce, Dr. Austin: 19

Pons, Lily: 86-88, 96
Princess Theatre Shows: 11, 44-46, 57, 63

Radio City Music Hall: 95
Ravel: 4
Remick: 30
Reynolds, Herbert: 43
Rio Rita: 69-70
Robeson, Paul: 77, 96
Rodgers, Richard: 9-10, 38, 108
Rodzinski, Artur: 96-98
Rogers, Ginger: 86
Rosenfeld, Monroe H.: 29-30
Rothafel, S. L.: 78
Rubens, Alma: 77
Rubens, Paul: 42

Sanderson, Julia: 39, 42, 43
Satie: 4
Schildkraut, Joseph: 77
Schubert, Franz: 4, 16
Schuberts, The: 41
Schwartz, Jean: 36
Scott, Randolph: 87
Segal, Vivienne: 57, 86
Seldes, Gilbert: 78
Shapiro and Bernstein: 31
Shaw, Artie: 89
Shaw, Oscar: 45
Shean, Al: 81
Shelley: 52
Shore, Dinah: 114
Show Boat: 4, 62-78; film versions, 77
Sieglinde von Hirschfield (dog): 89
Sinatra, Frank: 113
Skelton, Red: 115
Slezak, Walter: 81
Smith, Alison: 73
Song-pluggers: 32-33
Songs, popular: 6-9
South Pacific: 9
Spencer, Kenneth: 77

Index

Stern, Joseph: 31
Stevenson, Robert L.: 52
Stock market crash: 53
Stothart, Herbert: 61-62
Stover, Maud Ream: 76
Straus, Oscar: 39-40
Strauss, Johann II: 4-5
Stravinsky: 4
Sutton Place: 13
Swanson, Gloria: 86

Tamara: 82
Tashman, Lilyan: 56
Taylor, Deems: 110
Tchaikovsky: 94
Templeton, Fay: 82
Tennyson: 52
Terris, Norma: 71
Thomas, George H.: 33
Thomas, John Charles: 96
Thomson, Virgil: 98-99
Tin Pan Alley: 5-8, 37, 56, 96, 99;
    Kern's career in, 29-40; location,
    30-31; naming of, 29-30; song-
    plugging, 32-34; stifling atmos-
    phere, 7
Tony Pastor's: 31
Tours, Frank: 41
Truex, Ernest: 45
Truman, President: 110-111
Tucker, Sophie: 106
Twain, Mark: 67, 99-101

Union Square: 6, 31, 32, 37
Urban, Joseph: 57, 71

Van and Schenck: 56-57
Verdi: 4
Von Tilzer, Harry: 30-31, 34

Wagner: 91, 94
Warfield, William: 77
Washington: 70, 76
Watts, Richard, Jr.: 73
Werrenrath, Reinald: 81
Westley, Helen: 87
White, George: 57
Whiteman, Paul: 95
Whiting, Jack: 83
Wilde, Cornel: 86, 107
Winninger, Charles: 71, 77, 115
Winter Garden: 41
Witmark & Sons: 30, 31
Wodehouse, P. G.: 26-27, 46-47,
    49-50, 56-57, 67-68
Woollcott, Alexander: 15, 65, 95
World War II: 104-106
Wynn, Ed: 61

Youmans, Vincent: 38, 62

Ziegfeld, Florenz: 56, 58, 66-67,
    69-71
Ziegfeld Theatre: 69-71, 77